Spiritual Lightning

Also by Deacon Richard Eason
from EWTN Publishing:

*Spiritual Excellence: The Path to Happiness,
Holiness, and Heaven*

Deacon Richard Eason

Spiritual Lightning

Answering Your Call from Jesus to Master His Values

EWTN Publishing, Inc.

Irondale, Alabama

EWTN Publishing, Inc.

5817 Old Leeds Road, Irondale, AL 35210

Distributed by Sophia Institute Press, Box 5284, Manchester, NH 03108.

Sophia Institute Press is a registered trademark of Sophia Institute.

paperback ISBN 978-1-68278-385-6

ebook ISBN 978-1-68278-386-3

Library of Congress Control Number: 2024932577

First printing

For Rosalyn, Blake, Kyle, Grant, Ashley, Jenn, Evan, and Clare

Contents

Preface

Our Lord Jesus desperately wants every soul to get to Heaven. Along the way in our journey of life, Jesus touches every soul many times with His grace of *spiritual lightning*. This is a call to change our ways from a focus on earthly things—with its attachments, fears, stresses, worries, and false promises—to a focus on His mission assignment, which is for each and every one of us to follow His teachings in order to reach Heaven. If we accept this grace from Jesus, we experience His divine power which converts us to His way of life as one of His Holy Ones living in His spiritual Kingdom here on earth.

This book begins with the different ways the grace of spiritual lightning is used by Jesus to motivate each soul to answer His call. Then the reader is asked to identify the specific form of spiritual lightning utilized by Our Lord to touch their soul. Next, we analyze the lives of saints and ordinary people as examples to illustrate how spiritual lightning was unleashed in their souls. It continues with a study of the teachings Jesus called us to learn and follow to maintain this divine grace at work in our souls. Then there is a series of reflection questions for each of the teachings of Jesus. Lastly, we discuss how to develop a *master plan* to follow so you can answer the call from Our Lord to implement His teachings in order to reach Heaven.

This book is based on inspirations from the Holy Spirit, over two hundred Scripture quotations, teachings from more than twenty saints, encyclicals from the popes, several spiritual authors, and the *Catechism of the Catholic Church*. Some may regard it as a form of continuing spiritual education for our souls. The chapters are short, making it easy to learn and follow the teachings of Jesus. After all, He told us, ""I am the way and the truth and the life. No one comes to the Father except through me" (John 14:6).

Answering the call from Jesus *of spiritual lightning in your soul* is a game-changer that will lead you to an amazing life, which will help you and those around you reach Heaven. Please say *yes* to this call from Our Lord. We can't afford to miss this. Otherwise, we surrender ourselves to be consumed by earthly issues as influenced by the evil one.

Acknowledgments

The Holy Spirit is the true author of this work. Every word comes from Him. It is my hope that this work will inspire the souls who read it to fully accept the grace of *spiritual lightning* from Our Lord to change their lives and master the values of Jesus, thereby living a most joyful life. The values described herein were practiced daily by Jesus, His Blessed Mother Mary, and all the saints. Our Lord taught these values so we can bring an end to the life struggles that rob us of living an abundant life.

Thanks so much to all the people who helped shape my life so I could be totally open to the grace from God to put together this work. Thanks to my mother, Mary Eason, and my father, Rudy Eason, for their endless efforts in raising me in the practice of the Catholic Faith. Thanks to my wife, Rosalyn, for being a truly holy soul and for her numerous hours editing and improving this book. Thanks to our three sons, Blake, Kyle, and Grant; our daughter-in-law, Ashley; and our future daughter-in-law, Jenn, for their continued dedication to the practice of their Catholic Faith.

The motivation for this work was to inform my three sons, daughter-in-law, future daughter-in-law, and grandchildren Evan and Clare about the wonderful grace of spiritual lightning to answer the call from Jesus to master His values. By doing so, they can overcome any and all challenges they may experience in life and never ever struggle, as Our Lord is always there for them. It is my hope that all souls will answer this same call, live these values, and always experience a wonderful life.

Many thanks to Fr. Joe Krafft for his review of this book and his encouragement to help other souls understand the grace of spiritual lightning and how it can be a spiritual game changer for them. Much appreciation to Msgr. Christopher Nalty for his inspiration as my pastor at Good Shepherd parish and to Bishop Robert J. Baker Emeritus for his encouragement to spread the Good News of Jesus as an author. Thanks to Bob Stern, Dr. David Edwards, Jessie Pullins, and Tom Tucker for their willingness to share their stories of how the grace of spiritual lightning touched their souls. Thanks so much to Raymond Arroyo for all his help and guidance in pursuing the publication of this book. My gratitude to Nora Malone and Daniel Hopkins for their efforts in editing this work and to Devin Jones of EWTN for his guidance and encouragement throughout the publication process.

Much gratitude to Danny Abramowicz, Bishop Robert J. Baker, and Raymond Arroyo for their endorsements of the book. The photo for the cover is from a stained-glass window inside St. Patrick's Church in New Orleans, Louisiana. It was taken by Dominic Fayard with the permission of Fr. Garrett O'Brien, the pastor of the church.

Introduction

St. Patrick's Catholic Church, in the central business district of New Orleans, was built in 1840. In the rear of the church, on the right side, is a stained-glass window in which the artist depicts Our Lord Jesus pointing His finger at Saul (St. Paul) who is falling off his horse, struck down by this divine power—like a bolt of spiritual lightning. This encounter with Jesus inspired Saul to completely change his life from someone who persecuted Christians to a fervent disciple of Jesus (Acts 9). This conversion was so powerful that St. Paul is recognized as one of the apostles of Jesus, who wrote many books of the New Testament, spread the Good News across numerous countries, and was beheaded as a martyr in Rome.

I began going to noon Mass at St. Patrick's Church nearly forty years ago. It is located only a few blocks from my law office. It is a large church with numerous stained-glass windows. As guided by the Holy Spirit, I often sat next to the stained-glass window depicting the image of St. Paul and reflected on how this spiritual-lightning event dramatically changed his life forever. Over the years, I realized that spiritual lightning had struck my own soul, unleashing its divine power within. This grace inspired me to change my life and, as a husband, father, grandfather, lawyer, teacher, coach, and deacon, to live by the values Jesus taught.

As I reflected upon previous interactions with clients, witnesses, employees, parishioners, the homeless, nursing-home and hospital patients, family members, children, players, coaches, parents, teachers, seminarians, deacons, priests, professional athletes, and others, it became clear to me that many of them had been struck by spiritual lightning that inspired them to change their lives to follow the values of Jesus and to live abundant lives. Others were touched by spiritual lightning and failed to recognize it or totally ignored it. Oftentimes, in meeting with many of these individuals, we would inevitably discuss the image of St. Paul and how the divine power of spiritual lightning had caused a dramatic change in his life, thereby allowing him to experience joy, happiness, and peace by living the values of Jesus. We would further discuss the events of their lives and how the divine power of spiritual lightning had been unleashed in them by Jesus as a sign to change and to follow His ways.

I began praying to Jesus for His guidance as to whether He wanted a book written that would utilize Scripture as inspired by the Holy Spirit and encourage all souls to answer His call to unleash the divine power of spiritual lightning. I spoke with others about this idea, all of whom agreed it would help many souls. Further inspiration for this book comes from the prophet Ezekiel who wrote, "I will give you a new heart, and a new spirit I will put within you. I will remove the heart of stone from your flesh and give you a heart of flesh. I will put my spirit within you so that you walk in my statutes, observe my ordinances, and keep them" (36:26–27). St. Peter further writes, "There is no prophecy of scripture that is a matter of personal interpretation, for no prophecy ever came through human will; but rather human beings moved by the Holy Spirit spoke under the influence of God" (2 Pet. 1:20-21).

Jesus Christ left the joys of Heaven and willingly came into earthly life as our Savior for the purpose of leading every soul to Heaven. Our Lord wants no soul left behind. His love for us is immeasurable. Proof of this great love was demonstrated best when He laid down His life for us through His Passion and Crucifixion—the cruelest death possible.

To help every soul get to Heaven, Jesus sends us the grace of spiritual lightning at different times in our lives to get our attention. Our Lord tells us, "You call me 'teacher' and 'master,' and rightly so, for indeed I am.... I have given you a model to follow, so that as I have done for you, you should also do" (John 13:13, 15). Spiritual lightning comes in many ways: dramatically, circumstantially, and indirectly or subtly.

Dramatic spiritual lightning can be a major change in your life, such as a health issue, a spiritual experience, an accident, the loss of a family member or a close friend, a job loss or career change, or a family crisis. Circumstantial spiritual lightning can come in the form of a series of failures, achievements, occurrences, or events in your life. When spiritual lightning is indirect or subtle, grace can flow from being involved in a church ministry or a community activity, from guidance from a friend or mentor that helps solve a problem, from inspiration from reading a book, from achievement from a work project, or from a great experience with your spouse or another family member.

A wonderful example of dramatic spiritual lightning from Jesus occurred as He was hanging on the Cross. There were two criminals being crucified, one on both sides of Him. One responded to this moment of spiritual lightning from Our Lord during His suffering and asked Jesus, "Remember me when you come into your Kingdom." Our Lord responded: "Amen, I say to you, today you will be with me in Paradise." The other criminal ignored the spiritual lightning and missed the opportunity to reach Heaven (Luke 23:39-43).

Who are we going to be like? The saved criminal or the lost one? No one wants to be the soul that ignored Jesus' spiritual lightning and missed out on Heaven.

Are we paying attention and responding to this grace of spiritual lightning, or are we ignoring it? He is calling you! We can respond to this call to live an abundant life by learning and following the values He taught us during His public ministry on earth. By ignoring this opportunity, we subject ourselves to the attacks of the evil one, who is filling our souls with unnecessary doubts, earthly attachments, fears, worries, anxieties, and temptations.

Please don't waste another moment. Respond to His call and unleash God's divine grace of spiritual lightning in your soul. Let this great power run wild to allow your soul to live in a state of spiritual bliss. We no longer need to feel lost, bounced around like a ping-pong ball through life. St. Paul says that God chose each one of us "before the foundation of the world, to be holy and without blemish before him." He further explains that God "destined us for adoption to himself through Jesus Christ, in accord with the favor of his will" (Eph. 1:4-5).

The odds of getting struck by lightning in your lifetime are only 1 in 15,300. Similarly, there is a limited number of times when Jesus touches our souls with *spiritual* lightning. We can't afford to miss these wake-up calls. Unleashing this divine power is a spiritual game changer that leads us to an amazing life far beyond what we could ever imagine, and will guide us on the way to Heaven. St. Richard of Chichester wrote a wonderful prayer in 1254 that helps us with the concentration we need to unleash this divine power

of spiritual lightning in our souls so we can live the teachings of
Jesus and reach Heaven. He wrote:

> Thanks be to Thee, Lord Jesus Christ,
> For all the benefits Thou hast given me,
> For all the pains and insults Thou hast borne for me,
> O most merciful Redeemer—Friend and Brother,
> May I know Thee more clearly, love Thee more dearly,
> And follow Thee more nearly, day by day.

Part I

Identify the Call of Spiritual Lightning from Jesus That Touched Your Soul

A. Spiritual Lightning from Jesus Happens in Many Ways

One of the most powerful examples of the divine power of spiritual lightning involves St. Paul. In Acts 9, 22, and 26, we learn that Saul, as he was previously known, persecuted the early Christians, which led to their imprisonment and death. On one occasion, he was traveling to Damascus to bring back more Christians for imprisonment when he was struck by divine spiritual lightning, which blinded him. He heard a voice saying, "Saul, Saul, why are you persecuting me?" Saul asked, "Who are you, sir?" The voice replied, "I am Jesus, whom you are persecuting." The Lord then told Saul to go to Damascus for instructions on what to do (Acts 9:4-6).

In Damascus, a disciple of Jesus named Ananias came to Saul and said, "Saul, my brother, the Lord has sent me, Jesus who appeared to you on the way by which you came, that you may regain your sight and be filled with the holy Spirit" (Acts 9:17). Immediately, Saul regained his sight. Ananias further told Saul that God had designated him to know His will, to hear His voice, to be a witness to all that he had seen and heard, be baptized, and call upon His name. Saul stayed in Damascus and began to proclaim

Jesus in the synagogues. He confounded the Jewish leaders by his change of heart to serve God. He no longer persecuted the Christians but spread the Good News all over the region. This disciple became known as Paul, who wrote many of the books of the New Testament.

St. Peter speaks directly about God's use of divine power to help each soul live His values in order to escape the corruption of the world and reach Heaven. Peter wrote:

> His divine power has bestowed on us everything that makes for life and devotion, through the knowledge of him who called us by his own glory and power. Through these, he has bestowed on us the precious and very great promises, so that through them you may come to share in the divine nature, after escaping from the corruption that is in the world because of evil desire.... Therefore, brothers, be all the more eager to make your call and election firm, for, in doing so, you will never stumble. For, in this way, entry into the eternal kingdom of our Lord and savior Jesus Christ will be richly provided for you. (2 Pet. 1:3-4, 10-11)

The divine power of spiritual lightning touches souls in many ways: dramatically, circumstantially, and subtly or indirectly. Our Lord utilizes countless ways to touch each soul in one form or another as a wake-up call to change our lives.

B. An Individual Spiritual Self-Examination to Identify Your Call from Jesus

Jesus has impacted your life with the grace of spiritual lightning. It is time to perform a spiritual self-examination (SSE) to identify when and how He touched your soul by His call. We have listed many of these possible impacts that are based on personal experiences, descriptions from numerous others, or from spiritual writings—and Our Lord may have touched your soul in a way not listed here. Please set aside the time to do this SSE. It takes only ten to fifteen minutes. Open with prayer to Our Lord and seek His guidance in doing your analysis. Identify the form or forms of spiritual lightning from Jesus that have touched your soul from the possibilities listed below. You will be truly amazed at how Our Lord has been at work in your soul in ways you never imagined.

Dramatically

- ☐ A physical illness, such as COVID-19, cancer, heart disease, stroke, or another debilitating illness
- ☐ An accident: at work, in an automobile, at home, or from a product that caused personal injury or a disability
- ☐ A spiritual experience during prayer time, attendance at Mass, after Confession, or during a retreat
- ☐ A victim of a crime
- ☐ An event happens that leads you to return to the Church
- ☐ Loss of a close family member or a friend: spouse, parent, child, sibling
- ☐ An unexpected job loss or promotion
- ☐ The birth of a child or a grandchild
- ☐ Control of an addiction
- ☐ Conversion to the Catholic Faith
- ☐ A career change
- ☐ The startup of a new ministry

Circumstantially

- ☐ A series of failures or disappointments
- ☐ An overwhelming challenge or challenges
- ☐ A series of achievements

Indirectly or Subtly

- ☐ A meaningful conversation with someone close to you
- ☐ A treating physician advises you to alter your exercise, eating, or drinking habits
- ☐ A spouse asks you to direct more attention to your family
- ☐ A work superior encourages you in your job or asks you to modify certain work practices
- ☐ Grace from participation in a church ministry or community activity
- ☐ Guidance from a mentor
- ☐ Inspiration from reading a book
- ☐ Successful achievement in education or acquiring a professional license

In Other Ways

- ☐ _____
- ☐ _____
- ☐ _____
- ☐ _____

C. Stories of Saints and Ordinary People Who Answered the Call of Spiritual Lightning

There are many saints and ordinary people who have answered the call from Jesus by the grace of spiritual lightning to live His ways. They said *yes* to Jesus. St. Paul describes those who answered this call: "So then you are no longer strangers and sojourners, but you are fellow citizens with the holy ones and members of the household of God, built upon the foundation of the apostles and prophets, with Christ Jesus himself as the capstone" (Eph. 2:19-20).

Here are the stories of some of these wonderful role models.

St. Teresa of Ávila

Spiritual lightning struck St. Teresa of Ávila when she answered the call to leave her life as a rebellious teenager and to serve Our Lord as a religious and later to found a religious order.

St. Teresa of Ávila was born on March 28, 1515, in Ávila, Spain. Her original name was Teresa Sánchez de Cepeda Dávila y Ahumada. Her father was Alonso Sánchez de Cepeda, who was very strict and known as an honest man. Her mother was Beatriz de Ahumada y Cuevas.

This saint was a challenge to her parents as a teenager. Her focus was on clothes, flirting with boys, and being rebellious. Because of this conduct, her father sent her to a Carmelite convent. While there, her love for God began to grow. Spiritual lightning struck the soul of St. Teresa as she gave up the idea of married life and chose to be a religious.

While in the convent, St. Teresa developed mental prayer. Her focus was to keep Jesus present within her. At the age of twenty-two, she became ill with malaria, suffered from a seizure, and many thought that she would die. For the next three years, she was paralyzed. Her illness impacted her prayer life, and for many years she prayed very little.

St. Teresa gradually returned to her prayer life at age forty-one. During this time, she experienced raptures with God. Her body would levitate from the ground. In quiet prayer, she could sense God's presence. She learned to put God first in her life which gave her great peace and inspiration.

At age forty-three, the saint founded a new order, the Discalced Carmelites, that focused on a simple life of obedience, poverty, and prayer. She was highly criticized for her efforts. Eight years later, she began to spread a movement of reform, which was often met with great opposition. Her ideas spread throughout Spain and much of Europe.

Several books were written by her in which she describes her prayer life, contemplation, and her intimate relationship with God. In the book *The Way of Perfection*, the saint describes the importance of perfection. She wrote, "You already know that the cornerstone must be a good conscience that with all your strength you must strive to free yourselves even from the venial sins and seek what is the most perfect." She further described the power of God at work in our lives. She wrote, "Consider that He (God) can do all things, and we can't do anything here below but what He enables us to do."

In this book, the saint further describes the importance of keeping our attention focused on Jesus. She wrote, "Oh Lord, how true that all harm comes to us from not keeping our eyes fixed on You, if we were to look at nothing else but the way, we would soon arrive. But we meet with a thousand falls and obstacles and lose the way because we don't keep our eyes as I say on the true way." Additionally, she writes that each soul has a specific task to do for Our Lord. She states, "Thus, since the Lord knows what each one is suited for, He gives to each person a proper task, one that He sees as appropriate for that person's soul, for the service of the Lord Himself, and for the good of neighbor."[1]

---

[1] *The Way of Perfection*, in *The Collected Works of St. Teresa of Avila*, trans. Kieran Kavanaugh, O.C.D., and Otilio Rodriguez, O.C.D., vol. 2 (Washington, DC: ICS Publications, 2012), chaps. 5, 16, 18; see also "Teresa of Avila," Catholic Online, https://www.catholic.org/saints/saint.php?saint_id=208.

St. Ignatius of Loyola

While recovering from injuries sustained in a battle, St. Ignatius of Loyola was struck by spiritual lightning and answered the call to dedicate his life to serve Jesus and later start a religious order.

St. Ignatius was born on December 24, 1491, in Azpeitia in northern Spain. He was the youngest of thirteen children. His father, Don Beltrán, was the Lord of Oñaz and Loyola. Ignatius's mother died when he was seven years old, and he was raised by Maria de Garin, the wife of a blacksmith.

At the age of eighteen, he became a soldier where he learned discipline, obedience, and prudence. The saint participated in several battles under the leadership of the Duke of Nájera. As a result of his success, he commanded his own troops.

During a battle in 1521, St. Ignatius was struck by a cannonball, which severely injured his legs. He underwent several surgeries to save his legs, but his health declined, and he was advised to prepare for death. Part of one of his legs was amputated.

During his recovery from these injuries, the saint became an avid reader of stories about the saints. He also read a book titled *Vita Christi* (The life of Christ). It suggested a spiritual exercise to picture oneself in the presence of Jesus. From his personal studies, he recognized that he wanted to work for Jesus and convert non-Christians.

In 1522, spiritual lightning struck his soul, and the saint entered a Benedictine monastery. He began working in a hospital in the town of Manresa. In his spare time away from work, he frequently visited a cave where he developed the practice of Spiritual Exercises and later wrote the book *Spiritual Exercises*. This book helped people distinguish between the spirit of God and the evil one. These Spiritual Exercises are practiced today all over the world.

At age thirty-eight, Ignatius attended the University of Paris. While there, he became friends with Francis Xavier and Peter Faber, to whom he taught the Spiritual Exercises. The saint founded a group known as the "Friends in the Lord," who practiced these exercises. In 1540, the group was approved as a religious order by Pope Paul III. They became known as the Society of Jesus and later as the Jesuits.

St. Ignatius practiced strict discipline in the order. They focused their efforts on education. By the time of the saint's death in 1556, the order had one thousand members serving at thirty-five schools. The Society of Jesus made a strong effort to combat heresy.

The Jesuits are still known today for educating youth all over the world and have founded several universities.[2]

St. Vincent de Paul

Struck by spiritual lightning when he was kidnapped and held captive by pirates for two years, St. Vincent de Paul answered the call to help the poor and later founded a religious order dedicated to that very purpose.

St. Vincent was born in the town of Pouy in southwest France on April 24, 1581. His father was Jean de Paul, and his mother was Bertrande de Moras, who were both farmers. St. Vincent had three brothers and two sisters. He received his early education from the Cordelier Brothers, who were part of the Franciscan Order.

The saint began his college education at Zaragoza University in Spain and completed it at the University of Toulouse. He acquired

---

[2] "St. Ignatius of Loyola," Catholic Online, https://www.catholic.org/saints/saint.php?saint_id=56; see also Joseph Vann, ed., *Lives of Saints* (New York: John J. Crawley, 1954).

a doctorate in theology and was ordained a priest at the age of twenty-four.

In 1605, St. Vincent was sailing as a passenger when his ship was taken captive by Barbary pirates. He was kidnapped, sold as a slave, and resold several times to different owners. During this time, he prayed to our Blessed Mother Mary for her intercession and was able to escape to France in 1607.

In 1608, the saint moved to Rome, where he became a chaplain to the Count of Goigny. His duties in this position were to distribute money to the poor of the city.

At age forty-nine, St. Vincent moved to Paris to become a director at the College des Bons Enfants. While there, he developed a constitution and rules for the house. In 1632, the college became part of the priory of St. Lazare. They became known as the Lazarists and later as the Vincentians. This congregation founded by St. Vincent consisted of priests and laymen who took vows of poverty, chastity, and obedience. These men worked in missions, developed seminaries, and performed charitable deeds.

Thereafter, the saint began preaching missions to help the poor and build hospitals for them. To help accomplish this plan, he founded the Ladies of Charity, who collected money to aid this work. St. Louise de Marillac was one of the Ladies of Charity. St. Vincent and St. Louise founded the religious order known as the Company of the Daughters of Charity, who devoted their lives to serving the poor and the sick. There are more than eighteen thousand Daughters today serving in eighty-four countries.

Despite all of the challenges St. Vincent faced in his work in many endeavors, he maintained his focus on God and was able to keep his peace of mind. He freely accepted all of these events as the will of God and pursued perfection by means of self-denial, prayer, and being humble of heart.

The saint experienced much suffering at the end of his life. He was eighty years old when he died and was buried in the St. Vincent de Paul Chapel in Paris. He is considered the patron saint of charities and hospitals.[3]

St. Bernadette Soubirous

Struck by spiritual lightning through several apparitions of our Blessed Mother Mary, St. Bernadette Soubirous answered the call to become a religious in the Sisters of Charity.

St. Bernadette was born on January 7, 1844, in Lourdes, France, to François and Louise Soubirous. She had three younger brothers and a younger sister. Her father worked various types of jobs to support the family. Mrs. Soubirous was an excellent mother who was zealous in the practice of the Catholic Faith. Having a large family required St. Bernadette to do laundry work to earn money for the family. She helped raise her younger siblings and her duties included teaching them religion and Christian values.

At age fourteen, the saint began attending a school administered by the Sisters of Charity. During this time, she studied religion. The sisters observed that St. Bernadette had a wonderful personality.

On February 11, 1858, the saint came home from school and asked her mother if she could go to the Gave de Pau River with her younger sister, Toinette Marie, age nine, to gather firewood. They were joined by a neighborhood friend, Marie Abadie, age twelve. On the side of the river, there was a grotto known as Massabielle. Toinette and Marie waded across the river. Bernadette was standing by herself next to the river when a very beautiful Lady appeared

---

[3] "St. Vincent de Paul," Catholic Online, https://www.catholic.org/saints/saint.php?saint_id=326; see also Vann, *Lives of Saints.*

to her above a rosebush in the grotto. Bernadette fell to her knees and began to pray the Rosary. The Lady had a rosary and prayed with her. After finishing the Rosary, the Lady disappeared.

Seven days later, St. Bernadette returned to the grotto with two women from Lourdes. The Lady appeared to her again and asked her to come back on fifteen consecutive days. On each subsequent day, Bernadette saw the Lady.

On February 26, 1858, the saint went to the grotto. At the Lady's request, she uncovered a tiny spring of water coming from a rock. St. Bernadette drank the water and washed her face in it. The next day, water from the spring continued to flow into the river. Today, water from the spring continues to flow steadily into the river. Many people regard this as a miracle.

On March 2, 1858, the Lady told St. Bernadette to tell the priests in Lourdes to build a chapel. Three weeks later on March 25, 1858, the Lady again appeared to St. Bernadette, who asked her about her identity. The Lady responded by saying that she was the Immaculate Conception. The last apparition was on July 16, 1858.

When the saint was twenty years old, spiritual lightning struck her soul, and she entered the Sisters of Charity. During her training there, she did various jobs, including working in the kitchen, helping sick people in the infirmary, and later doing assignments in the sacristy. In all these assignments, she demonstrated great humility and a great desire to serve.

St. Bernadette was asked if she experienced pride because the Blessed Mother appeared to her. Her response was that Our Lady picked her only because she was the most ignorant.

The saint remained in the convent of the Sisters of Charity in the motherhouse in Nevers. She continued to work in the infirmary and in the sacristy. She was diagnosed with tuberculosis in her knee and later died at age thirty-five on April 16, 1879, while praying the Rosary. Her last words were, "Blessed Mary, Mother of God, pray for me. A poor sinner. A poor sinner."

There have been many miracles performed at the grotto in Lourdes, France. Seventy have been verified by the Lourdes Medical Bureau.[4]

Ordinary People

Bob Stern

Spiritual lightning struck Bob Stern, and he answered the call from Our Lord to convert from Judaism to the Catholic Faith and is now in formation to be a deacon.

Bob was born in 1958 in Metairie, Louisiana, to Ralph and Mae Stern and was raised in the Jewish faith. After graduation from college, he married his wife, Charlene. They are blessed with two children and seven grandchildren. Bob works in the wealth management business. He was a member of a synagogue in New Orleans from childhood and for most of his adult life. He attended services there twice a year.

In 2015, Bob was inspired by the Holy Spirit to attend a Catholic retreat at the Manresa Retreat House in Convent, Louisiana, to get closer to God. He contacted them but was told the retreat was full and they had no place for him. Bob was not discouraged, as he felt the call to attend the retreat, so he went there anyway, and they found a room for him.

On the first day, the retreat master, Fr. Callahan, spoke about talking to Jesus as a friend. In pondering this message that day, Bob walked on the Mississippi River levee across from the retreat house for an entire hour, talking to Jesus for the first time in his

---

[4] Vann, *Lives of Saints*.

life. Later that day, he opened the New Testament and began to study the Bible. Bob repeated the same activity on the next two days of the retreat.

The experience at the Manresa retreat turned his soul on fire in a way that he had never known before. This spiritual experience taught Bob that Jesus is not just a prophet but is truly Our Lord and Savior. As Bob was waking up the morning after the retreat, he felt the presence of Jesus touching him. This left him totally scared and overwhelmed. He prayed to Jesus, telling Him of his love for Him, but he needed some space. On a walk that night, he asked Jesus to come back into his life. The next weekend, he attended Mass with his family.

Over the next year, Bob pondered all these events. He returned to Manresa for a second retreat. During his stay there, spiritual lightning struck his soul, and he decided to convert to the Catholic Faith. He started attending RCIA in October 2016. Over the next six months, he chose not to shave and grew a beard, vowing that on the day of his admission into the Church, he would shave for the last time as a Jew. Bob was brought into the Church during the Easter Vigil Mass in 2017.

Bob began attending Mass at Immaculate Conception Parish in New Orleans. He became very active in ministry there as a lector and as a Eucharistic minister at Mass and bringing the Eucharist to patients at Ochsner Hospital. He read many spiritual books to continue to grow in his faith.

In 2021, he began discerning the call to be a deacon. While attending a Sunday Mass, the parish bulletin had a notice about a meeting for those interested in the diaconate. Bob and Charlene attended the meeting. From that meeting, Bob answered the call to pursue the diaconate and is now in formation. He is a member of the class of 2027.

Spiritual Lightning

Dr. David Edwards

Spiritual lightning struck Dr. David Edwards, and he answered the call from God to rely upon his faith and the great support of his family to overcome a health crisis from a rare debilitating disease.

Dr. David was born in Fort Campbell, Kentucky, to LTC Steven and Jill Edwards (now Eaton). He was raised in the Methodist Church but didn't practice his faith there.

In his early years of college, Dr. David was focused on going to school and partying with his fraternity brothers. During this time, he began dating Megan Coney, who was a practicing Catholic and had a clear vision for her future. She helped Dr. David refocus his attention on his future and consider conversion to the Catholic Faith. After dating for about six months, they broke up.

But Dr. David was called by God to convert to the Catholic Faith. He began dating Megan again, and they later married. He completed his education and now practices as a doctor of chiropractic medicine. They have four children.

In the summer of 2017, Dr. David developed various neurological symptoms, including the loss of feeling in his arms. The condition threatened his ability to practice as a chiropractor and greatly impacted his family life. He was depressed over his future.

Diagnostic testing was performed and reviewed by four prominent neurosurgeons from various parts of the country who were in agreement that the most likely diagnosis was a tumor on his spine. The preliminary diagnosis was possible cancer, which might require very risky spinal surgery.

In search of the proper treatment for this condition, Dr. David went to the Mayo Clinic in September 2018. He saw a team of physicians who diagnosed his condition as neurosarcoidosis. He underwent ten months of high-dose corticosteroid treatments and has been cured. Dr. David did not have to undergo the risky spinal surgery, as originally discussed. This type of surgery almost certainly would have left him with neurological symptoms.

Over the two years from the onset of his symptoms until his condition resolved, Dr. David learned to answer the call from God and rely upon his faith and the great support of his family. Megan and Dr. David prayed to Ashley Code—a young lady from Metairie, Louisiana, who had died of a brain tumor in 2016 at age seventeen—asking her to intercede with Our Lord for a cure of this crippling disease. Because of his faith and family help, Dr. David was able to overcome the temptations to despair and to substance abuse. Without the support of his faith and his family, he would have succumbed to fear, anxiety, and depression. Megan and Dr. David attribute the correct diagnosis, treatment, and remission of the disease to the intercession of Ashley Code with Our Lord Jesus Christ.

Jessie Pullins

Spiritual lightning struck Jessie Pullins, and he answered the call from God to give up a life of drugs and homelessness to live a spiritual life helping others overcome these same obstacles.

Jessie was one of seven children born to Bernice and Horace Pullins. He served six years in the U.S. Army in various positions as a tank operator, a scout, and a truck driver and in the infantry. During the Cold War in Europe, he served two years on the border between East and West Germany.

After leaving the army in 1979, Jessie had a hard time adjusting to civilian life. Over the next ten years, he went to trade school, studying automotive and diesel mechanics, and worked at various jobs, mostly through a temporary agency. During this time, he became addicted to drugs. One night, he considered suicide while standing on the top of the Claiborne Avenue Bridge. A voice told him not to jump, as he wouldn't die but would instead become disabled.

Over the next eight years, Jessie became homeless. He slept in front of the New Orleans Public Library on a cardboard box. At times, he would stay overnight in various homeless shelters. He pushed a basket, scrapped cans for money, ate out of a dumpster, and battled his drug addiction.

In the late 1990s, Jessie was convicted of burglary of a car and spent eighteen months in jail. After being discharged in 2000, he returned to street life.

Spiritual lightning struck Jessie when he realized he had to see his parole officer or face more jail time. To see him, he had to be drug free, but he still had illegal substances in his system. At that time, he needed a hernia operation and decided to have the surgery because he thought this would help him become clean. When he woke up in the recovery room following the surgery, Jessie knew this was the beginning of the rest of his life. He asked God for help.

After leaving the hospital, his addiction crept back into his life. Jessie had a choice to turn left, where he had access to dope, or go right, to where the Ozanam Inn homeless shelter was located. Our Lord guided Jessie to the inn, which became his sanctuary until he could control his addiction. Jessie has been sober and drug free since he made this decision.

He learned in his recovery that "God will do for you what you can't do for yourself, if you allow Him to work in your life."

Jessie began working as a custodian and climbed his way up to the chief steward at the JW Marriott Hotel. Four years ago, he left the hotel business to start his own company in the scrap industry and renting bicycles. Jessie owns his home. He is married to Lorraine Pullins.

Since spiritual lightning struck his soul, one of Jessie's biggest goals in life has been to help others who have addictions or are homeless, or both. He has served on the board of Unity of Greater New Orleans, which provides housing to the homeless. He works on the Homeless Collaboration Plan with the New Orleans Police Department to help those on the street to reach shelters. Every other week, he teaches a class at the Ozanam Inn, sharing his story and offering ideas to help men and women get back on their feet and lead productive, happy lives.

Tom Tucker

Spiritual lightning struck Tom Tucker, and he answered the call from Jesus to minister to teenagers and others by handing out crosses and telling them all about the love Jesus has for them and to rely upon Him for all their decisions.

Tom was born in 1941 to Gertrude and Raleigh Tucker in Evansville, Indiana. He is one of nine children. His father died at the age of thirty-three when Tom was only six years old. The Tucker family was of limited means, but his mother always said that they were so blessed because they had their faith and their family. Tom is married to Chris, and they have three children and nine grandchildren.

Tom responded to the call to enter the seminary in ninth grade at St. Meinrad in southern Indiana. After three years, his stepfather passed away, so he left the seminary to care for his mother and his siblings.

For many years, Tom was a Sunday Catholic going through the motions of his spiritual journey without any true defined purpose. He attended a Cursillo Retreat, where spiritual lightning touched his soul. Our Lord guided him to work in youth ministry. Through various activities and talks in ministry work, he taught young people the values of Jesus. In doing this work, he handed out a cross to each student as a reminder to them that Jesus loves them and that they should rely upon Our Lord to make all their decisions.

Tom's practice of handing out crosses was not limited to students. He gave them to his friends, to people on the street, and to parishioners in many churches. His message was constant: that Jesus loves every soul all the time. He has handed out hundreds of crosses through all of these different avenues.

A few years ago, there was a gathering for Tom's birthday. One of the students he worked with previously in ministry was there that night. The former student spoke in front of all the attendees, explaining that he had been suffering from substance abuse. He further said that the cross Tom gave him helped him in making many life decisions and to overcome his addiction because he knew that Jesus loves him. There are many other former students who later in life reminded Tom that carrying the cross he gave them helped them make major life decisions.

As Tom matured in his faith, the reception of the Eucharist at Mass became most meaningful to him. He proclaims to many souls that the Eucharist is the true Body and Blood of Jesus and that it helps to keep them spiritually strong. The Eucharist energizes his mission to spread the Good News to others.

For many years now, Tom has conducted a weekly prayer group at his home. At each meeting there is prayer, a discussion of Scripture or a spiritual book, and fellowship. Tom and his wife, Chris, recently went to the Holy Land on a pilgrimage, which he described as the spiritual journey of a lifetime. Tom said this was a fantastic opportunity to walk in the footsteps of Jesus. The pilgrimage confirmed to Tom his message to others that Jesus loves every soul all the time.

Part II

Learning to Master the Values Taught by Jesus in His Public Ministry

Now that you have performed your spiritual self-examination as to how Jesus touched your soul by His grace of spiritual lightning, and have reviewed the lives of saints and ordinary souls, you *must* answer the call from Jesus to change your life to learn and master the teachings He taught in His public ministry on earth. The whole purpose for Jesus coming to earth as the Messiah was to incite everyone with His values, to follow His teachings to a new way of life, to revolt against sinful ways, and to reform our lives in order to get to Heaven. We can't ignore this call and continue to open ourselves to the actions of the evil one, who fills our souls with unnecessary doubts, fears, worries, and temptation. Each one of us is at the dawn of opportunity to experience lasting joy, happiness, and peace that will lead us to Heaven.

Some of you may be thinking about why it is so important to learn the values of Jesus. Our Lord greatly desires us to do so. In fact, He is referred to as "Teacher" over fifty times in the Bible. Mark's Gospel states, "When he disembarked and saw a vast crowd, his heart was moved with pity for them, for they were like sheep without a shepherd; and he began to teach them many things"

(6:34). Moreover, at His Last Supper on earth, Jesus spoke about many of these values to the apostles, as this was His final time to be with them in this life. He specifically told them, "You call me 'teacher' and 'master,' and rightly so, for indeed I am.... I have given you a model to follow, so that as I have done for you, you should also do" (John 13:13, 15). When He rose from the dead and made several appearances to the apostles, He continued teaching them. We can't let His life, Passion, and Crucifixion be for nothing.

The vast majority of Catholics complete their formal religious education by age eighteen. As a consequence, there is a huge gap in our spiritual knowledge. It is critical to fill this gap to make the divine power of spiritual lightning become fruitful, leading us to an abundant life. Very specifically, we must immerse ourselves in learning to master the values that Jesus taught during His public ministry, to become one of His beloved disciples. From His early life in Nazareth to His death in Jerusalem, Our Lord taught us these values that will get us to Heaven if we learn and follow them. As Jesus says in the Gospel, "I came so that they might have life and have it more abundantly" (John 10:10). St. Paul further instructs us to grow in our spiritual knowledge: "Let the word of Christ dwell in you richly" (Col. 3:16).

This book addresses the core teachings of Jesus that we all need to follow so that we may fully unleash the divine power of Jesus in our souls. With each of these teachings comes a grace from God. These values are: following the two major commandments from God, walking away from temptation and sin, listening to the voice of Jesus, having faith (a necessity), living in a state of divine peace and maximizing the joy in your life, becoming a catalyst for Jesus, receiving the Eucharist and going to Confession (which are the highways to Heaven), having devotion to our Blessed Mother, having prayer time as the most important part of your day, modeling our families after the Holy Family, managing suffering and death, experiencing the healing power of Jesus, and reaching the only true goal in life — Heaven.

Following teaching 15, see the reflection questions for each of these teachings.

Teaching #1

Love God without Limits

Grace from God: Replacing our will with His will

My Aunt Vivian and Uncle Rob met a little later in life, in their forties, and were married. They had a wonderful life together, helping their families, working hard, taking trips, and spending all of their free time with one another. Their true love had no limits.

Aunt Vivian was diagnosed with Alzheimer's in her seventies and was confined to a nursing home for several years. This disease was not an impediment to Uncle Rob's love for her. He went to see her every day, often bringing homecooked meals that he made for her. As my aunt's disease progressed, she didn't even recognize Rob. At times, she thought he was a stranger and asked him to leave her room. My uncle never wavered in his love for Vivian. He came to visit her every day until she passed. His love for Vivian had no limits.

At the time of Jesus, there were 613 laws to follow in the Jewish faith. There were 248 do's and 365 don'ts. The Jewish leaders of the time were frequently debating which of the 613 laws was the greatest. In Matthew's Gospel, Our Lord simplifies the 613 laws into two commandments for His disciples to follow. These two commandments focus on love without limits, with the greatest being first. Jesus says, "You shall love the Lord, your God, with all your heart, with all your soul, and with all your mind" (Matt. 22:37).

So what does this commandment really mean? It means that our every thought, word, and action comes from Jesus, always doing His will and never our will. Furthermore, we must have a total commitment to Him with no earthly distractions of temptation, selfishness, fear, or stress. We are called to love God above everyone and everything. Jesus is the way of life for our souls.

To comply with this commandment, we must build a relationship with Our Lord in a similar way that we have with our spouse, a best friend, or close family member. To build this relationship with Him, we must spend time with Our Lord every day in prayer. This is easy when you think about it. We can pray for a few minutes when we wake up in the morning, ask God for His guidance during the day, at lunchtime reflect on the morning activities, and seek His will for us in the afternoon. At the end of the day, spend time alone with Our Lord, thanking Him for all of the blessings of the day, seeking His forgiveness for ways that we may have sinned against Him, talking with Him about any concerns we have, and seeking His will for us for the next day.

There are other ways to fulfill this commandment of love for God. We can study and meditate on the Bible, participate in a prayer group, attend Mass regularly, receive the Eucharist, and spend time in Adoration.

Sr. Suzanne Anglim, a religious in the Daughters of Charity, has spent nearly sixty years in ministry work as an educator, visiting the sick in hospitals, and helping the poorest of the poor in homeless shelters. Over these many years, she has worked in poverty areas in St. Louis, Los Angeles, El Paso, and New Orleans. Sr. Suzanne told me that her best friend in life is Jesus and that she spends time with Him every night. She relies upon Our Lord for guidance and direction throughout her daily activities.

Building a relationship with Jesus is not a new invention. The apostles and saints did it, and so do priests and religious. So why not us? After all, Jesus brought us into this life. He is our Creator and deserves the very best that we have to give every single day. Our relationship with Him must be first in our lives. He must come before all else.

Many people think it is impossible to have a relationship with Our Lord. They don't want to be bothered, offering up lame excuses, such as being too busy with daily activities. They can't miss their television shows or Facebook time. In the time of Moses, God spoke about the lame excuses made by the people. They complained that His idea was too difficult to understand or it was all pie in the sky (Deut. 30:11-12).

It is most important to know that our soul naturally desires this love from Jesus, but often we get in the way. Sometimes we are our own worst enemies. Knowing that the most important goal in life is to gain Heaven, can we really rely upon these lame excuses to forgo this special opportunity?

There is another way to think about this issue. When Jesus calls us from this life, our earthly business successes, leisurely activities, possessions, and time on our cell phones and watching television will mean absolutely nothing. By stark contrast, having a great relationship with Jesus through prayer and doing His will gives us a chance to reach the most important goal in this life—finding *eternal* life in Heaven.

The apostle John wrote about his relationship with Jesus and the commandments:

The way we may be sure that we know him is to keep his commandments. Whoever says, "I know him," but does not keep his commandments is a liar, and the truth is not in him. But whoever keeps his word, the love of God is truly perfected in him. This is the way we may know that we are in union with him: whoever claims to abide in him ought to live [just] as he lived. (1 John 2:3-6)

Our Blessed Mother Mary describes her commitment to this commandment in Luke's Gospel: "Behold, I am the handmaid of the Lord. May it be done to me according to your word" (1:38). Our Lady fully committed to the love of God without any limits.

Jesus spoke about the importance of honoring this commandment. In the Gospel according to John, He told the apostles, "If you keep my commandments, you will remain in my love, just as I have kept my Father's commandments and remain in his love" (15:10). Our Lord emphasizes the importance of the basics of our Faith in honoring His commandments.

Jesus Himself was the greatest role model for His commandment of love of God by spending His whole earthly life loving God His Father with all His heart, soul, and mind. Leaving His family to travel the region to help others, with only a cloak on His back, showed us that He loved us more than Himself. He fulfilled God's mission assignment wonderfully by being an obedient child to our Blessed Mother Mary and St. Joseph, teaching His apostles and disciples the ways of God His Father, being a caregiver, and performing miracles to those afflicted with disease and curing them. Ultimately, He gave up His life for us by His Crucifixion.

The apostle John wrote, "Whoever is without love does not know God, for God is love" (1 John 4:8). St. Paul describes this love as "the bond of perfection" (Col. 3:14).

The secular world is trying to take God's commands out of our lives. They want us to ignore and forget Him. There are many examples of this: prayer is gone from public institutions; the Ten Commandments have been removed from parks, schools, and courthouses; mass shootings and gun violence have become commonplace; and media outlets and politicians promote hatred of others as normal behavior. God is being replaced in our lives with the evil one and his awful ways. Many of us can fall prey to this onslaught—the attack on Christian values. We can get to the point where we only take Jesus out of a box in our souls for an hour or so at Mass. We return Him to that box when we leave church only to go back to being influenced by the evil one. We can never forget that our whole being was created by God. We owe Him our very existence, every heartbeat and every breath we take. Simply stated, we owe Jesus the love He commands from us.

By keeping this commandment from Jesus and having a relationship with Him, we will experience divine peace and joy. St. Paul says, "Have no anxiety at all, but in everything, by prayer and petition, with thanksgiving, make your requests known to God. Then the peace of God that surpasses all understanding will guard your hearts and minds in Christ Jesus" (Phil. 4:6-7).

Bl. Fr. Miguel Pro was born in 1891 into a mining family. He became a Jesuit priest who lived in Mexico City. In 1917, the Mexican government passed anti-Catholic laws that prohibited priests from ministering publicly. The actions of the government didn't stop this priest from pursuing his ministry, fulfilling God's commandment to him to love the Lord with all his heart, soul, and mind. He went underground, performing his priestly duties, often wearing disguises to hide himself. He celebrated Mass in private homes and provided the poor with food, clothing, and shelter. He was arrested by the government and was ordered to be executed by firing squad. He faced his executioners with a crucifix in one hand and a rosary in the other, imitating Our Lord as He was crucified, and shouted these words: ¡*Viva Cristo Rey!*—"Long live Christ the King!"[5]

By living God's commandment, our love for Him must be without any limits. In the same way that He committed Himself to us, we must commit ourselves to Him. This kind of love is truly the bond of perfection. It will ensure us of living an abundant life on earth, doing His will and reaching Heaven.

Spiritual Treasures for Reflection

You shall love the Lord, your God, with all your heart, with all your soul, and with all your mind. (Matt. 22:37)

The way we may be sure that we know him is to keep his commandments. Whoever says, "I know him," but does not keep his commandments is a liar, and the truth is not in him. But whoever keeps his word, the love of God is truly perfected in him. This is the way we may know that we are in union with him: whoever claims to abide in him ought to live [just] as he lived. (1 John 2:3-6)

Whoever is without love does not know God, for God is love. (1 John 4:8)

---

[5] "Who Was Blessed Miguel Pro?," Bl. Miguel Pro Catholic Academy, https://miguelpro.org/blessed-miguel-pro/

Teaching #2

Love Your Neighbor as Yourself

Grace from God: Being selfless as a way of life

In 2005, Hurricane Katrina struck the New Orleans area, causing catastrophic damage to this community, including the loss of over one thousand lives and billions of dollars in property damage. In the aftermath of the storm, major flooding remained in the city, leaving thousands of citizens stranded in their homes without water and food in sweltering conditions. Government services were unable to handle the rescue missions. The Cajun Navy, a volunteer flotilla, came to help their neighbors. Hundreds of people in boats gathered in Cajun country near Lafayette, Louisiana. These volunteers came to the city and rescued thousands of folks trapped by the floodwaters. The Cajun Navy continues to answer the call for help in south Louisiana, assisting victims of storms when needed. These men and women truly carry out their goal of helping their neighbors in need.

Our Lord said this is the second greatest commandment: "You shall love your neighbor as yourself" (Matt. 22:39). He further explained this commandment when He said, "Love one another. As I have loved you, so you also should love one another" (John 13:34).

Following this commandment requires us to learn to be selfless, not selfish. This term is defined as being concerned more with the needs and wishes of others than of oneself. Being selfless, serving others, was Our Lord's constant motivation in His public ministry. Jesus left His family home and lived in poverty, spreading the Good News to others, helping them grow spiritually, desperately trying to get them all to heaven. He preached using parables, fed five thousand people, cured thousands from demons and disease, and raised some from the dead. Most importantly, He demonstrated great compassion for others, leaving no soul behind.

Jesus taught the apostles about the importance of being selfless in Mark's Gospel. The apostles James and John spoke with Jesus one day as they were traveling to Jerusalem. They told Jesus that they wanted to sit next to Him in Heaven, one on His right side and the other on His left. The other ten apostles reacted to this request by becoming indignant toward James and John. Jesus explained, "Whoever wishes to be great among you will be your servant; whoever wishes to be first among you will be the slave of all" (Mark 10:43-44).

Our Lord emphasized His teaching about this commitment to be selfless when He said, "No one has greater love than this, to lay down one's life for one's friends." (John 15:13). Jesus freely gave up His life to save all of us.

St. Thérèse of Lisieux describes this commitment as one of the requirements to be a saint. She wrote that to be a saint, one has to deny your very self, always seek out the most perfect thing to do, and be willing to suffer much.[6]

---

[6] *Story of a Soul: The Autobiography of Saint Thérèse of Lisieux*, 3rd ed., trans. John Clarke, O.C.D. (Washington, DC: ICS Publications), 27.

So, who is my neighbor? Jesus explains this in Matthew 25:31-46. When the Son of Man comes at the end of time, He will separate everyone into two groups—just as a shepherd separates the sheep from the goats. He will place the sheep on His right who were selfless and the goats on His left who were selfish. The selfless on His right will be awarded Heaven. He said to them, "For I was hungry and you gave me food, I was thirsty and you gave me drink, a stranger and you welcomed me, naked and you clothed me, ill and you cared for me, in prison and you visited me" (vv. 35-36). The self-righteous goats question Jesus about *when* they saw Him hungry, thirsty, a stranger, naked, ill, or in prison and didn't tend to Him. The Lord said to them, "Amen, I say to you, what you did not do for one of these least ones, you did not do for me" (v. 45). Our Lord told them that they will go off to eternal punishment.

This message from Jesus to help others as if they were Our Lord in disguise sets forth the Corporal Works of Mercy: to feed the hungry, give drink to the thirsty, shelter the homeless, visit the sick, visit prisoners, bury the dead, and give alms to the poor.

Jesus gave us a great example of living by this commandment when He helped the outcasts and the marginalized such as a leper. At that time, lepers were not allowed to mix in with the general population. They were thought to be sinners and impure. They were considered to be very contagious, capable of easily transmitting the disease to others. Lepers had to label themselves by shaving their heads and warning others of their presence, shouting, "Unclean, unclean!" Not only did Jesus meet with this leper, He helped him by performing a miracle of curing him of this dreaded disease (Luke 5:12-14).

To be a true disciple of Jesus requires that we live by this commandment. He tells us this directly: "This is how all will know that you are my disciples, if you have love for one another" (John 13:35).

How are we to fulfill this commandment in the world today? There are obvious people we can help and some who are not so obvious. The obvious folks are the homebound and the elderly in our families and neighborhoods. We can give them some of our time by cooking for them, shopping for their needs, and checking on them by a simple phone call. As to the homeless standing at intersections in our communities, we can offer them water or nutritious food. Our son Kyle works as a volunteer for Habitat for Humanity to help build homes for needy families and provides guidance to them on basic finances so they can live successfully in these properties.

The less obvious people to help include coworkers who have been bullied or marginalized by others in the company. Develop a relationship with them to learn about their families, and include them in gatherings. Others to help are neighbors and friends who have been discriminated against because of their ethnicity, race, or appearance, or for other reasons. Get to know them and include them in community, ministry, or social gatherings. Don't overlook family members who have been mistreated. We can show them respect and help them build trust in us. Encouraging others to discontinue any practices of mistreatment will help to alleviate this problem. There are simple tasks as well, such as driving courteously on the highway or offering others a place in line before us.

This commandment from Jesus to care for others is not always easy. At times, we are challenged and have to extend ourselves to care for a sick child, parent, or spouse. Sometimes it can be difficult to work with a coworker who is hard to communicate with or who is mean-spirited. St. Catherine of Siena said that Our Lord spoke to her about this challenge. She wrote, "I have placed you in the midst of your fellows so that you may ... love your neighbor ...

without expecting any return from him, and what you do to him I count as done to Me."[7]

Our American culture today promotes hatred as a way of life, just the opposite of the commandment from Jesus. Hatred means ill will toward others. It comes in many forms, such as discrimination based on skin color, appearance, level of education, type of job, amount of income, or sexual orientation. It can occur in other ways, such as being mean-spirited in what we say and do to family and friends, lying to gain an advantage in business or in a relationship, abusing others on social media, engaging in misconduct to our gain and loss to others, and bearing false witness against someone.

We can expect at times to be victims of hatred for our religious beliefs. This hatred can happen from being pro-life, choosing not to go along with the crowd, not pursuing wrongful acts, or just by spreading the Good News to others. Our Lord spoke about this issue when He said, "Because you do not belong to the world, and I have chosen you out of the world, the world hates you" (John 15:19).

At times we can grow weary of the ongoing hatred in our culture. The Good News is that we don't have to let this misconduct influence our joy in life. We all have a choice to make each day. Are we going to succumb to the ways of the world of hatred? Or are we going to serve Jesus by loving our neighbor as ourselves? We can reject these awful influences by the daily practice of unlimited love for Jesus and for others.

St. Mother Teresa of Calcutta is one of the great role models of our time who lived by this commandment. In 1948, she founded

---

[7] Fr. Conley Bertrand, S.T.D., *Understanding the Sunday Gospels, YEAR A*, 140.

the religious order Missionaries of Charity to help the needy in her country. She dedicated her life to this cause. One of the vows of the order is to give "wholehearted free service to the poorest of the poor." Her dedication to her mission is best exemplified by her expression, "I must be willing to give whatever it takes to do good to others. This requires that I be willing to give until it hurts." This saint was awarded the Nobel Peace Prize and gave the funds from the award to the poor.[8]

The benefits of following this commandment are unlimited grace from Jesus. All of us have experienced the great delight that enters our hearts when we help others. It is a wonderful feeling knowing that God is working through us. The apostle John sums up the importance of doing what Our Lord requests of us: "No one has ever seen God. Yet, if we love one another, God remains in us, and his love is brought to perfection in us" (1 John 4:12).

Since we know that God's love for us is without limits, we must honor His command to us to love our neighbor as ourselves. Being selfless by always helping others far outweighs the earthly pleasures that come from selfish conduct. All Jesus asks of us is to follow His example in public ministry, leaving no soul behind.

---

[8] "'Give Until It Hurts': The Christian Wisdom of Mother Teresa in 9 Quotes," *Christian Today*, September 5, 2017, https://www. christiantoday.com/article/give-until-it-hurts-the-christian-wisdom-of-mother-teresa-in-9-quotes/113084.htm.

Spiritual Treasures for Reflection

You shall love your neighbor as yourself. (Matt. 22:39)

Love one another. As I have loved you, so you also should love one another. (John 13:34)

Whoever wishes to be great among you will be your servant; whoever wishes to be first among you will be the slave of all. (Mark 10:43–44)

Teaching #3

Eliminate Temptation and Sin from Your Life

Grace from God: Returning to joy, happiness, and peace

One of the great sporting events in the United States is the Kentucky Derby, held in Louisville on the first Saturday of May each year. In this race, there are numerous horses competing for the grand prize of more than $1,800,000. It has been labeled as the most exciting two minutes in sports. Some of the past winners are Secretariat, Seattle Slew, and American Pharaoh. As many as 155,000 people attend this event in person, and millions more watch on television. With as many as twenty different horses in the race, there is intense competition to win this event.

In our lives, there is also an intense competition. It is the race for our souls. There are two competitors in this race: God and the evil one. God gives us His virtues of faith, hope, charity, prudence, justice, courage, and temperance. The other competitor offers the temptations of selfishness, pride, lust, jealousy, laziness, hatred, slander, substance abuse, gluttony, and impure thoughts. The key question is who is going to win this race for our souls. Is it going to be God's will at work in our souls or the evil one with his temptations?

Jesus spoke of this competition when He was in the Garden of Gethsemane with His apostles. He asked them to stay awake with Him for an hour as He prayed to God His Father about His upcoming Passion and Crucifixion, but selfishness and laziness overcame them, and they all fell asleep. He said to the apostle Peter, "The Spirit is willing, but the flesh is weak" (Matt. 26: 41). Sometimes the temptations of this world prevail in us against the will of God.

Psalm 95 provides us with clear motivation to choose God's will in this race. We want to avoid His wrath. The psalmist wrote, "Do not harden your hearts as at Meribah, as on the day of Massah in the desert. There your ancestors tested me; they tried me though they had seen my works. Forty years I loathed that generation; I said: 'This people's heart goes astray; they do not know my ways.' Therefore I swore in my anger: 'They shall never enter my rest'" (Ps. 95:8-11).

Contractors working on a construction project use all kinds of tools on the job. Plumbers use wrenches and pipes, electricians work with cutting devices and wire, and carpenters utilize hammers and wood. These tools are required to complete their work successfully.

To ensure that God's will is the winner in the race for our souls, we have several tools available to us to eliminate temptation and sin. These tools are: virtues, self-discipline, a daily examen, a daily scorecard, and Confession.

Virtues

A virtue is defined as a habitual and firm disposition to do good. It allows a person to give the best of himself. The *Catechism of the Catholic Church* tells us that the virtuous person chooses to do good in all his actions (CCC 1803-1804). There are different types of virtues.

The theological virtues are faith, hope, and charity. They relate directly to God and allow us to live in a relationship with the Holy Trinity. These virtues are the foundation of Christian moral activity. They are infused into our souls to help us act as God's children and reach eternal life in Heaven (CCC 1812–1813).

The cardinal virtues are prudence, justice, fortitude, and temperance. Prudence allows us to determine true good in all circumstances and gives us guidance to select the right way of achieving it. Justice disposes men to respect the rights of others to pursue the common good. Fortitude strengthens us to overcome temptations and enables us to conquer fear and face trials and persecutions. Temperance provides mastery over pleasure and helps us control our desires (CCC 1805–1809).

During the recent pandemic, there was a rush by the government and big pharma to develop a vaccine to provide immunity against the dangers of COVID-19. The goal of this effort was to prevent the spread of this disease, which killed over one million Americans and disabled hundreds of thousands of others. Virtues are like spiritual vaccines. By practicing God's virtues, we develop a spiritual immunity to temptation and sin, which prevents the loss of our soul.

God gives us grace to overcome temptation and sin. He gives us the grace necessary to persevere in the pursuit of the virtues (CCC 1811). We can ask Our Lord and Savior for it in prayer.

Self-Discipline

A second tool available to us is self-discipline. This term is defined as the ability to overcome our weaknesses and to pursue what is right despite any temptation to abandon it. Self-discipline is required for success in all aspects of life. It is a fundamental requirement in military service and a must for success in sports and business.

In raising children, parents frequently discipline their children. They do not do it with a mean heart but the sincere desire for their children to learn the values of Jesus to help them live an abundant, productive life in order to gain Heaven. As our children grow up and reach adulthood, hopefully they have learned to practice self-discipline to fulfill God's mission assignment for them. Without self-discipline, they fall prey to the desires of the evil one that leads to a life of misery and uncertainty.

After Our Lord's Crucifixion, St. Peter became the first pope of the Church. He practiced self-discipline in all aspects of his life. The saint described this concept in his first letter in the New Testament: "Like obedient children, do not act in compliance with the desires of your former ignorance but, as he who called you is holy, be holy yourselves in every aspect of your conduct" (1 Pet. 1:14–15).

After Jesus was baptized in the Jordan River, He went into the desert for forty days to fast. He was tempted by the devil several times. He was able to defeat the temptations by self-discipline and grace from God. Jesus was first tempted to make bread out of stones to overcome His hunger. Then the devil offered Jesus power over all the kingdoms of the world in exchange for His commitment. Finally, the devil urged Jesus to throw Himself off the top of the temple to be caught by God's angels. These temptations were intended to persuade Jesus to give up His mission from God to be the Messiah.

Daily Examination

Another tool to overcome temptation and sin is to perform a daily examination of our conscience as taught by St. Ignatius of Loyola. In this process we evaluate our performance in serving Our Lord each day. Start with recognizing that you are in God's presence.

Then think about all the blessings He provided to you during the day. Next, recall when God was present for you in all the events of the day. Then identify any sins you committed, express sorrow for them, and ask for His forgiveness. Finally, seek grace from God for all your actions for the next day.[9]

After a few days of engaging in a daily self-examination of conscience, we will become aware of repetitive sinful conduct, which will be embarrassing for us. We will be forced to take action to terminate our sinfulness. For this, we can use a daily scorecard.

Daily Scorecard

Keeping a daily scorecard of our sins is an effective way to battle temptation and sin. Scorecards are used to track the performance of participants in a sport to determine their success. In baseball, a scorekeeper records runs, hits, and errors. In golf, a record is kept of the number of strokes per hole.

In our spiritual life, we can keep a daily scorecard of our sins. By tracking our transgressions, we will strengthen our consciences to resist future temptations. After a week or ten days of recording our sins, it will become obvious that we need to amend our lives and put on a new self. St. Paul describes the process this way: "You should put away the old self of your former way of life, corrupted through deceitful desires, and be renewed in the spirit of your minds, and put on the new self, created in God's way in righteousness and holiness of the truth" (Eph. 4:22–24).

Below is a sample scorecard to use for a ten-day period to shed temptation and sin from your life. Keeping a scorecard only takes a few minutes each day. Try it for ten days, and you will be amazed

---

9   "The Ignatian Examen," Jesuits, https://www.jesuits.org/spirituality /the-ignatian-examen/.

at the difference this can make in your joy and happiness in life. By the end of each day, simply check the sin(s) that you committed.

Sins	1	2	3	4	5	6	7	8	9	10
Lust										
Pride										
Anger										
Gluttony										
Envy										
Greed										
Laziness										
Substance abuse										
Slander										
Selfishness										
Impure thoughts										
Other:										

——————————

——————————

——————————

The Sacrament of Reconciliation

Another tool to consider is the Sacrament of Reconciliation, or Confession. This important sacrament is often forgotten or over-looked. It is easy to offer an excuse not to participate in it, by thinking that it's too hard to contemplate all the aspects of our sinfulness and then to confess these sins to a priest. It is not easy to acknowledge our weaknesses. But make no mistake, the rewards of peace and grace from Our Lord following Confession far outweigh any perceived challenge.

A true conversion of our souls happens when we participate in this sacrament on a regular basis, such as monthly. An examination of our souls often reveals repetition of the same sins. Confessing the same transgressions over and over again is an embarrassment. It is an admission that we don't have the self-discipline to eliminate them. We can cure these repetitious sins with grace from Our Lord. A sincere confession will instill great peace in our hearts, knowing that our sins have been forgiven by the mercy of God. Forgiveness of our sins and mercy from God are real. Our Lord, as well as His saints and our popes, have confirmed this. All we have to do is make a sincere confession.

During Our Lord's ministry on earth, He gave us a prayer to say to His Father to help us overcome temptation. In the Lord's Prayer, we ask God, "Do not subject us to the final test, but deliver us from the evil one" (Matt. 6:13). Don't kid yourself! There is a war raging among the evil forces fighting for our souls. This is often described as spiritual warfare. Mother Angelica describes it this way: "The devil may not get your soul, but he will use every means possible to decrease your degree of glory in the Kingdom. He will watch, and wait, and determine your weakest point, and then he will work on that. This is the strategy of the enemy."[10]

When we engage in sin, we separate ourselves from God. This causes us to experience anxiety, worry, fear, and stress. All of these symptoms are preventable by practicing the tools against temptation. When we utilize these tools, we can defeat sin and enjoy a return to joy, happiness, and peace. We can ensure that God will win the race for our souls.

---

[10] Raymond Arroyo, ed., *Mother Angelica's Little Book of Life Lessons and Everyday Spirituality* (New York: Doubleday, 2007), 152.

Spiritual Treasures for Reflection

The spirit is willing, but the flesh is weak. (Matt. 26:41)

Like obedient children, do not act in compliance with the desires of your former ignorance but, as he who called you is holy, be holy yourselves in every aspect of your conduct. (1 Pet. 1:14–15)

You should put away the old self of your former way of life, corrupted through deceitful desires, and be renewed in the spirit of your minds, and put on the new self, created in God's way in righteousness and holiness of truth. (Eph. 4:22–24)

Teaching #4

Listen to the Voice of Jesus

Grace from God: Continuous guidance and direction in our lives

In the fall of each year, millions of fans gather together to watch football games all across America. The games are played on many levels—from the professionals, colleges, high schools, and playgrounds. Many would agree that the most important player in the game is the quarterback. He gathers all eleven offensive players on the field into a huddle. In there, all the players listen to his voice as he calls a play that directs them to perform a specific assignment. The players break the huddle and line up on the field. Then the quarterback barks out the signals and directs the center to hike the ball to him, starting the play. For the play to be successful, all eleven players must listen carefully to the voice of the quarterback in the huddle and to his signals and then perform their assignments.

For us to have success in our spiritual journey in life, we must learn to listen to the voice of our spiritual quarterback—Jesus. Following His commands leads us to an abundant life in Heaven. Without daily direction from Our Lord, we become confused, make poor decisions, commit sins, and are lost in this life. God, our Father, specifically tells us to listen to the voice of His Son Jesus. When Peter, James, and John were on Mount Tabor, Jesus was transfigured into His divine being. At that time, God said, "This is my chosen Son; listen to him" (Luke 9:35).

In chapter 10 of John's Gospel, Jesus confirms the importance of learning to listen to His voice. He tells us that He is the Good Shepherd who is there to guide our souls at all times through His messages to us so that we might have life and have it more abundantly. We are His sheep whom He calls by name. As our Good Shepherd, He will lay down His life for us. Jesus tells us directly that, "My sheep hear my voice; I know them, and they follow me. I give them eternal life, and they shall never perish. No one can take them out of my hand" (John 10:27–28). Jesus further tells us that there is a competing voice for our souls—from the thief, the evil one, who seeks to steal, slaughter, and destroy us. We will run away from this stranger because we do not recognize his voice (John 10:3–5, 7–11).

One of the greatest stories in the Bible about the importance of listening to the voice of Jesus comes from Saul, who later became the apostle Paul. One day, when Saul was on his way to Damascus to find Christians to persecute, he was struck by spiritual lightning and blinded. He heard a voice saying, "Saul, Saul, why are you persecuting me?... I am Jesus, whom you are persecuting. Now get up and go into the city and you will be told what you must do (Acts 9:1–6).

Men accompanying Saul brought him to Damascus. For three days, he was unable to see. A man named Ananias, a disciple of Jesus, was told by the voice of Our Lord to go to the house of Judas to see Saul. The Lord further said to him, "Go, for this man is a chosen instrument of mine to carry my name before Gentiles, kings, and Israelites." Ananias obeyed Jesus and went to the house, saying to Saul, "Saul, my brother, the Lord has sent me, Jesus who appeared to you on the way by which you came, that you may regain your sight and be filled with the holy Spirit." Thereafter, Saul regained his sight and strength (Acts 9:7-18). Paul fulfilled Jesus's will for him, spreading the Good News everywhere, both orally and in writing fourteen books of the New Testament. Paul learned to listen to the voice of Jesus for all his future actions.

The apostle Paul wrote in his letter to the Hebrews, directing the disobedient to listen to the voice of Jesus and not to their own hearts. He wrote, "Oh, that today you would hear his voice: 'Harden not your hearts'" (4:7).

Before Jesus came into the world as our Messiah, several books of the Old Testament tell us about listening to the voice of God. In the First Book of Samuel, chapter 3, there is a story about Samuel, who was a minister of the Lord under the high priest Eli. One day, Samuel was sleeping in the temple. The Lord called to him, and Samuel ran to Eli and said, "Here I am. You called me." But Eli said he did not call him and told Samuel to go back to bed. This happened a second time in the same manner. A third time, the Lord called Samuel while he was sleeping, and he went to Eli. This time, Eli understood that the Lord was calling the youth. Eli told Samuel that if you are called by God, respond this way: "Speak Lord, for your servant is listening." When Samuel was sleeping again, the Lord called him. Samuel answered, "Speak, for your servant is listening" (1 Sam. 3:1-10).

A psalm written by David refers to the voice of the Lord in many different ways. You can hear it over waters. The voice of the Lord is power, splendor, cracks cedar trees, strikes with fiery flame, shakes the desert, makes deer dance, and strips the forests bare (Ps. 29:1-9).

There is no doubt that the greatest being who ever lived on earth was our Savior Jesus Christ. The four Gospels record many of the events of His three-year public ministry. There are numerous references in them where Jesus listened to the voice of God for guidance and direction for His actions.

In one instance, a woman who had been caught in adultery was brought by some scribes and Pharisees before Jesus. They argued that the woman should be stoned to death according to the Law of Moses. Before Jesus responded, He paused, writing on the ground with His finger, probably seeking guidance from the voice of God. Then He said to the accusers, "Let the one among you who is without sin be the first to throw a stone at her." In response, the Pharisees and Jews left the scene (John 8:3-9).

During His public ministry, Jesus went off by Himself frequently to listen to His Father. By His example, Our Lord gave us clear direction to listen to His Father's voice. If even Jesus sought guidance and direction from God, then why shouldn't we do the same? We have absolutely no excuse not to.

Our Lord teaches us about the importance of listening to His voice for direction and avoid becoming preoccupied by earthly worries. The Gospel of Luke describes the story of a visit by Jesus to the home of Mary and Martha. When Our Lord was there, Mary sat beside Him, listening to Him speak. Meanwhile, Martha was preoccupied with serving Jesus. Martha complained to Our Lord, asking Him to instruct Mary to help her. Jesus said in reply, "Martha, Martha, you are anxious and worried about many things. There is need of only one thing. Mary has chosen the better part and it will not be taken from her" (Luke 10:41-42).

St. Ignatius of Loyola writes about the power of listening to the voice of God and how it should consume our hearts: "It is true that the voice of God, having once penetrated the heart, becomes strong as the tempest and loud as the thunder." He explained that the voice can be blotted out by distractions if we let it. The saint further wrote, "Before reaching the heart, it is as weak as a light breath that scarcely agitates the air. It shrinks from noise and is silent amid agitation."[11]

There are many avenues available to us for the purpose of learning to listen to the voice of Jesus. Adoration before the Blessed Sacrament is excellent. Many priests, religious, and laypeople around the world spend an hour each day engaged in this practice. Another way is to find a quiet place in your home with a picture of Our Lord nearby. Whether by Adoration or in a quiet place at home, engage in conversation with Our Lord in the same way you would with your spouse or a close family member. He will speak with you genuinely if you seek His counsel. This one-on-one time with Jesus is awesome.

Spiritual reading is another way that Our Lord speaks to us. Perhaps the best way is to spend time studying the Bible. Select one of the Gospels and read one half-chapter at a time, meditating on the verses and writing down the thoughts that come to your mind in a journal. In this way, the messages from Jesus through His direct quotes and parables will touch your soul with guidance and direction. Reading books by Christian authors and reflecting on them in the same way is a great practice as well.

Rote prayers are effective as well in helping us to listen to the voice of Our Lord. Praying the Rosary and meditating on the life of Jesus will provide discernment for challenges you may face. Sometimes Our Lord communicates to us through circumstances and events that happen in our lives as well.

---

[11] Bishop Thomas J. Olmsted, "The Voice of Jesus: First in a Series," *Catholic Sun*, February 19, 2020, https://www.catholicsun.org /2020/02/19/the-voice-of-jesus-first-in-a-series/.

Each day, we have a choice of the voice we are going to listen to in simple actions. Is it going to be Jesus the Good Shepherd, or will it be the evil one? For example, suppose you are at the dinner table with your family, and your five-year-old son accidentally spills a glass of milk that makes a huge mess. The voice of the evil one tells you to get angry and yell at him. However, the voice of Jesus says, "Be patient, clean up the spill, and encourage your son to be more careful." Or suppose that one of your friends tells you and others about an award that she received. The voice of the evil one encourages your pride to surface and brag about one of your accomplishments. The voice of Jesus says, "Praise your friend for a job well done and never speak about yourself." The voice of Our Lord is there for us in everyday circumstances if we are listening to Him.

Listening to the voice of Jesus can guide us in making good decisions in challenging matters as well. As a deacon, I am often asked about difficult family situations. On one occasion, a brother asked me about a situation where he was a victim of slander. His sister told other family members behind his back that he had stolen money. The story wasn't true. When the brother learned about it, he was furious. The voice of the evil one told him to deny the allegation, retaliate against his sister, and hold a grudge against her. The voice of Jesus told the brother to clear his name in his family, put aside the grudge, and forgive his sister.

We all have many tough decisions to make as we go through life. There are issues such as: changing jobs, handling a marital problem, disciplining a child for misconduct, mistreatment by a family member or a friend, healthcare decisions, and so on. There is a simple process to follow to listen to the voice of Jesus and make good decisions about all our actions. St. Ignatius of Loyola developed Spiritual Exercises to help us in this effort:

+ *Pray*: Recognize God's presence in all of your actions and pray throughout the day. By conducting yourself this way, you will be able to seek guidance from Jesus in making difficult decisions.
+ *Consider the different sides of the issue*: Make a list of pros and cons. Weigh each side of the issue. Consider the advice of other people you trust for their advice about the choice. Also, consider any moral implications.
+ *Imagine the impact of your final decision*: Consider the impact of your decision. If you are uncomfortable, revisit it. Then repeat the foregoing steps.
+ *Execute your choice*: Have faith that God has guided you in the process to make the proper choice, and execute it.
+ *Evaluate your decision*: You probably made a good decision if you feel a sense of confidence after you executed it. Consider whether your relationship with God and others is better or worse because of the choice you made.[12]

Constant communication with Our Lord by listening to His voice is available 24-7. We always have access to His comfort, guidance, and advice. We don't need to text or e-mail Him. All we need to do is immerse ourselves in our relationship with Him through Adoration time, one-on-one reflection time, spiritual reading, prayer time, or seeking advice from others. We can put our lives on autopilot with Jesus at the controls. Consistent communication and patient efforts with our Savior always bring incomparable wisdom, joy, and virtue. Without constant communication with Jesus by listening to His voice, we rob ourselves of divine guidance

---

[12] Ave Maria Press, "St. Ignatius of Loyola and Making Good Decisions," *Engaging Faith Blog*, https://www.avemariapress.com/engagingfaith/st-ignatius-loyola-and-making-good.

and are subject to the perils of misconduct, poor decision-making, and harmful behavior.

In our world today, there are countless distractions that pull us away from the voice and teachings of Jesus. Social media, television, video games, computers, cell phones, newspapers, and movies are examples of many things which can lead us astray and to listen to the wrong voice. The goal of the evil one is to steal, slaughter, and destroy us. The Good Shepherd, Jesus, is there to lead us to Heaven. All we have to do is listen to His voice for clear direction in all our thoughts, words, and actions.

Spiritual Treasures for Reflection

My sheep hear my voice; I know them, and they follow me. I give them eternal life, and they shall never perish. No one can take them out of my hand. (John 10:27–28)

Oh, that today you would hear his voice: "Harden not your hearts." (Heb. 4:7)

It is true that the voice of God, having once penetrated the heart, becomes strong as the tempest and loud as the thunder. (Bishop Olmsted, "The Voice of Jesus: First in a Series")

Teaching #5

Faith Is a Necessity, Not an Option

Grace from God: End of doubt in our souls

In my senior year of college, I felt the Lord was calling me to the vocation as a lawyer. Gaining admission to law school required a qualifying score on the Law School Admission Test (LSAT). I studied for several weeks in preparation. I took the test on a Saturday morning and was convinced that I had bombed it. I stayed out late on Saturday night with the thought that my future was shot. Where was Jesus when I needed Him? My faith was in total doubt. I came home around 4:00 a.m. and remembered that I was the lector scheduled for the 7:00 a.m. Mass at St. Clement of Rome Church. The Gospel reading that early morning was the story about Thomas, the doubting apostle. I am sure that reading on that day was no coincidence.

On the day Jesus rose from the dead, He appeared to the apostles in the upper room of a house in Jerusalem, with Thomas missing. When Thomas returned, the apostles explained to him that Our Lord had risen from the dead and appeared to them. Thomas had no faith that Jesus had resurrected from the dead. Several days later, when Thomas was in the upper room with the other apostles, Jesus appeared to them again. He said to Thomas, "Put your finger here and see my hands, and bring your hand and put it into my side, and do not be unbelieving, but believe." Thomas answered and said to him, "My Lord and my God!" Jesus said to him, "Have you come to believe because you have seen me? Blessed are those who have not seen and have believed" (John 20:24–29).

After listening to the Gospel that Sunday morning, I realized what an idiot I was for questioning my faith. A few weeks later, the LSAT test results came back with a qualifying score, and I was accepted into law school. This event reminded me that faith is a necessity and *not* an option.

Just as Our Lord taught me to have faith in Him about a vocation, He explained how important faith is for us. Jesus says, "Amen, I say to you, if you have faith the size of a mustard seed, you will say to this mountain, 'Move from here to there,' and it will move. Nothing will be impossible for you" (Matt. 17:20). He further says, "Everything is possible to the one who has faith" (Mark 9:23).

There can be a little "Doubting Thomas" in all of us. To help us overcome these concerns, Our Lord provides examples of direct and circumstantial proof that He is real and continues to be there to help us reach Heaven.

Direct proof is demonstrated by the many earthly appearances Jesus made after His Resurrection. As mentioned previously, He appeared to the apostles in the Upper Room three days after He was crucified (John 20:19–23). Subsequently, He walked with two disciples on the road to a small town outside Jerusalem known as Emmaus and had a meal with them (Luke 24:13–35). He ate breakfast with some of His apostles on the shore of the Sea of Tiberias after the apostles had fished all night (John 21:1-14). And Our Lord called the apostles together on Mount Olivet and ascended into Heaven before their eyes (Acts 1:6-12).

Through the many miracles Jesus performed in His public ministry, He gives us further direct proof of His desire that we reach Heaven. He healed the sick, cast out demons, fed five thousand people, and raised the dead. One of the most compelling miracles performed by Jesus was raising Lazarus from the dead.

Our Lord was friends with Lazarus and his two sisters, Martha and Mary. He heard that Lazarus had died and went to Judea to see him. When He arrived, Martha said to Jesus, "Lord, if you had been here, my brother would not have died. [But] even now I know that whatever you ask of God, God will give you." Jesus replied, "I am the resurrection and the life; whoever believes in me, even if he dies, will live.... Do you believe this?" Martha said, "Yes, Lord. I have come to believe that you are the Messiah, the Son of God, the one who is coming into the world." (John 11:21-22, 25-27).

Jesus wept over the loss of Lazarus. He went to the tomb where His friend was buried. Jesus said, "Take away the stone." Martha told Jesus, "Lord, by now there will be a stench; he has been dead for four days." But they removed the stone. Our Lord cried out in a loud voice, "Lazarus, come out!" Lazarus came back to life and walked out of the tomb (John 11:38-44).

Jesus appeared to St. Teresa of Ávila. She wrote, "One day, while I was in prayer, Jesus was so kind to show me His hands. They were so beautiful that I do not know how to describe them.... A few days from then I saw His divine face and I was left completely enraptured.... The Lord showed Himself to me little by little, given that He had to give me grace in order to see Him entirely.

However, I understand that it suited my natural weakness to happen this way. May He be forever blessed!"[13]

There are numerous examples of circumstantial proof that Jesus is real. Each one of us can point to our own personal experience, such as the miracles of the birth of our children and grandchildren; cures for health issues we may have suffered, such as cancer, heart disease, and orthopedic issues; obtaining that much-needed job to take care of our family; and daily guidance in challenging decisions.

Jesus offers support for those who believe based on circumstantial proof without direct proof. He says, "Blessed are those who have not seen and have believed" (John 20:29).

Pope St. Paul VI wrote in simple terms that faith in Jesus is to be the focal point of our lives. In the pastoral constitution *Gaudium et Spes*, he wrote, "The Lord is the goal of human history, the focal point of the longings of history and of civilization, the center of the human race, the joy of every heart and the answer to all its yearnings."[14]

Evidence that faith is a necessity in our lives was demonstrated best when Jesus went back to His hometown of Nazareth after beginning His public ministry. He sincerely hoped to be able to help His people, but He was rejected and was unable to do any mighty deeds there. They viewed Jesus as a lowly carpenter's son. He spoke about their lack of faith, saying, "A prophet is not without honor except in his native place and among his own kin

---

[13] Joseph Pronechen, "These Saints Had Visions of Heaven and Hell and Revealed What They Saw," *National Catholic Register*, December 2, 2022, https://www.ncregister.com/blog/saints-who-saw-heaven-and-hell.

[14] Second Vatican Council, Pastoral Constitution on the Church in the Modern World *Gaudium et Spes* (December 7, 1965), no. 45.

and in his own house" Our Lord was amazed by their lack of faith (Mark 6:1-6).

There are many characteristics of faith that confirm that it should be at the center of our human existence and *not* an option:

+ *All things are possible*: Jesus tells us, "Everything is possible to one who has faith" (Mark 9:23). St. Paul amplifies the message of Jesus when he says, "I have the strength for everything through him who empowers me" (Phil. 4:13).

+ *Faith brings about healing*: Jesus healed a woman who had been suffering from a blood disease for many years. She was treated by many doctors without success. Because of her faith, she touched Our Lord's cloak, believing that by touching His clothes, she would be cured. Jesus told her, "Daughter, your faith has saved you. Go in peace and be cured of your affliction" (Mark 5:34). Also, Elizabeth, the cousin of Our Blessed Mother Mary, who was thought to be unable to have a child, gave birth to John the Baptist (Luke 1:5-25).

+ *Faith produces perseverance*: The apostle James wrote that faith produces perseverance, which we all need for the difficult times in our lives. He wrote, "For you know that the testing of your faith produces perseverance" (James 1:3). Similarly, St. Paul wrote in his letter to Timothy, "Compete well for the faith" (1 Tim. 6:12).

+ *Faith is required when challenges arise*: One night, a violent storm developed on the sea, swamping the boat occupied by the apostles and Our Lord, who was sleeping at the time. The apostles woke Him, saying, "Lord, save us! We are perishing!" Jesus responded, "Why are you terrified, O you of little faith?" Then He got up, calmed the seas, and stopped the wind. The apostles were amazed and said, "What sort of man is this, whom even the winds and the sea obey?" (Matt. 8:23–27).

All of us are on the spectrum of faith. On one end are those of us who criticize and reject Jesus and work against Him, thereby following the evil one. Another group falls in the middle with limited faith that wavers back and forth based on personal situations. We can have doubts when faced with the loss of a job, health issues, family matters, or financial issues. We say, "Why me, Lord?" Sometimes we turn our back on Jesus, abandoning our faith and wondering if the crisis will work out. When life is rolling along smoothly, our faith is fine. Finally, there are those who have unwavering faith in God, where no matter what happens, their lives operate on autopilot with Jesus at the controls.

A study of the apostles reveals their progression along the spectrum of faith to 100 percent unwavering trust in Jesus. The apostles had limited faith in Jesus during the three years they were with Him in His public ministry. After Our Lord was crucified, this limited trust was replaced by fear. Then Our Lord appeared to them in the Upper Room and blessed them with the Holy Spirit, which transitioned the apostles to a state of faith on autopilot. Their trust in Jesus zoomed to the top. In fact, their faith became so strong that nearly all of them were martyred for their beliefs.

The first pope of the Church was one of the apostles who made this transition. During Our Lord's public ministry, St. Peter, who had a strong personality, often acted impulsively. Remember, he doubted Jesus, sank in the water, cut off the ear of a soldier, and denied knowing Our Lord three times. After receiving the Holy Spirit at Pentecost, St. Peter became the rock of faith upon which the early Church was built. He transitioned from denying Jesus to being a leader in spreading the Good News of Our Lord. For his evangelization efforts, he was crucified upside down.

Many of us today are in a state of transition somewhere between having limited faith in Jesus and allowing our souls to operate on autopilot with unwavering trust in Him. Sometimes we allow ourselves to be influenced by fear, worry, and doubt. It is truly time for each of us to complete the transition process and to be a rock for Jesus in our families, in our workplaces, and among our friends and neighbors. In all of our thoughts, words, and actions, we need to keep our focus on Him and on doing His will exclusively.

It is most important to recognize that living our lives on autopilot with 100 percent faith in Jesus comes with a great benefits package. Our Lord will be there for us in all of our problems, dilemmas, and challenges. He will bless us with His saving power in spiritual, physical, psychological, social, and emotional matters. Jesus always answers our prayers in His time, not in ours. He knows each one of us and what our needs are, and He will provide for them.

By our life experiences, it is easy to realize that faith in Jesus truly is a necessity. The time we act alone only leads to heartache and misery. My personal experience with the Law School Admission Test was positive proof of this fact for me. If we think about it, all of us have experienced similar situations. To know that all things are possible, healing power is accessible to us, and that there is help for us in troubled times—these are more than enough reasons to never view trust in Jesus as an option but as a necessity.

Spiritual Treasures for Reflection

Everything is possible to one who has faith. (Mark 9:23)

For you know that the testing of your faith produces perseverance. (James 1:3)

Compete well for the faith. (1 Tim. 6:12)

Teaching #6

Divine Peace Is the Remedy for Fear, Stress, Anxiety, and Worry

Grace from God: Living an abundant life

Adam and Eve were the first people on earth and had total dominion over it. They settled in the Garden of Eden. God instructed Adam, "You are free to eat from any of the trees of the garden except the tree of knowledge of good and evil. From that tree you shall not eat; when you eat from it you shall die" (Gen. 2:16-17). The serpent was in the garden and encouraged Eve to eat fruit from the forbidden tree. So she ate it and gave some to Adam, who ate it as well. Immediately, their eyes were opened, they realized they were naked, and they made loincloths for themselves (Gen. 3:1-7).

Later in the day, they heard the Lord God in the garden, and they hid themselves. God called to Adam, "Where are you?" Adam replied, "I heard You in the garden; but I was afraid, because I was naked, so I hid" (Gen. 3:9-10). God punished Adam and Eve, requiring them to toil for food and subjecting them to death (Gen. 3:16-24).

Adam and Eve introduced fear, stress, anxiety, and worry into the world by their misconduct. They totally ignored the will of God in favor of their own will. These symptoms have plagued man from their time down through the centuries and still today.

God sent His Son Jesus into the world to bring divine peace as the remedy for fear, stress, anxiety, and worry. Our Lord wants every soul to live in a continuous state of divine peace. Isaiah prophesied that Jesus would come into the world as the Prince of Peace. "For a child is born to us, a son is given to us; upon his shoulder dominion rests. They name him ... Prince of Peace." (Isa. 9:5). Indeed, Jesus came into the world, preaching peace during His public ministry. He frequently spoke to the apostles of its importance, especially at the Last Supper before His Crucifixion, and in the upper room on the night of His Resurrection. At the Last Supper, Jesus said, "Peace I leave with you; my peace I give to you. Not as the world gives do I give it to you. Do not let your hearts be troubled or afraid" (John 14:27).

Jesus was crucified the day after the Last Supper. He rose from the dead three days later and appeared to the apostles in the Upper Room. They were in a total state of fear, wondering if they would be crucified as well. Jesus knew how afraid they were. His first words to them were, "Peace be with you." After showing them His hands and His side, Jesus said to them again, "Peace be with you" (John 20:19–21). Our Lord helped them overcome their anxieties and worries by His appearance and His statements.

How do we gain divine peace in our souls to eliminate fear, stress, anxiety, and worry? There is a simple four-step process to follow:

1. *Identify the issue(s).* Take the time to identify the issue that is causing your heart to be troubled and fearful. It may be a family

matter, a health concern, a job situation, a financial obligation, misconduct, or another matter.

2. *Have 100 percent faith in Jesus.* During His public ministry, Jesus often spoke about the importance of replacing worry with faith in Him when challenges arise. In Luke's Gospel, Jesus was speaking to a large crowd when He spoke these words:

> Can any of you by worrying add a moment to your life-span? If even the smallest things are beyond your control, why are you anxious about the rest? Notice how the flowers grow. They do not toil or spin. But I tell you, not even Solomon in all his splendor was dressed like one of them. If God so clothes the grass in the field that grows today and is thrown into the oven tomorrow, will he not much more provide for you, O you of little faith?... Do not be afraid any longer, little flock, for your Father is pleased to give you the kingdom. (Luke 12:25-28, 32)

The apostle Peter emphasizes this message from Our Lord. He wrote, "Cast all your worries upon him because he cares for you" (1 Pet. 5:7).

3. *Practice courage in challenging times.* Courage — or fortitude — is a virtue that is defined as enabling one "to conquer fear, even fear of death, and to face trials and persecutions" (CCC 1808). It is a gift of the Holy Spirit (see Isa. 11:2). The first pope of the Church, St. Peter, learned firsthand how to have courage in a challenging time. One evening when the apostles were sailing on the Sea of Galilee several miles from the shore, high winds and waves began to swamp the boat. Suddenly, Jesus began walking on the sea toward them. The apostles were terrified. They thought it was a ghost. Jesus spoke to them, "Take courage, it is I; do not be afraid." Peter

replied, "Lord, if it is you, command me to come to you on the water." Jesus said, "Come." So, Peter got out of the boat and began to walk on the water. But as fear overcame him, he started to sink. Immediately, Jesus reached out and caught Peter (Matt. 14:27–31).

On the stormy sea that night, Peter experienced both fear and courage. When he had courage and faith, he was able to walk on the water. Peter's fear caused him to sink. It was only when he replaced courage with fear in his soul that he began to struggle. Focusing all of our attention on Jesus, having courage and faith in Him, is the difference between struggling in the waves of life or managing them as they occur.

4. *Submit the issue in prayer to Our Lord.* St. Paul tells us in his letter to the Philippians that, through prayer, Jesus will guide us when these challenges arise. He wrote, "Have no anxiety at all, but in everything, by prayer and petition, with thanksgiving, make your requests known to God. Then the peace of God that surpasses all understanding will guard your hearts and minds in Christ Jesus." (Phil. 4:6–7).

Our Lord utilized this simple process when He faced His greatest challenge on earth: His Passion and Crucifixion. After the Last Supper, Jesus was filled with fear. The issue was that He was going to be arrested based on a bogus charge and would be brutally tortured to death. He went to the Garden of Gethsemane to pray to His Father. He spoke to God in prayer, seeking guidance and direction. Our Lord had 100 percent faith that His Father would give Him the grace to manage this extreme suffering. He demonstrated phenomenal courage in the face of His coming Passion and Crucifixion.

Before Our Lord's Ascension into Heaven, He commissioned the apostles to start His Church. He instructed them to make disciples of all nations, baptizing them and teaching them His ways (Matt. 28:16-20). Each one of them faced many seemingly impossible challenges as they complied with Jesus' command. They traveled all around the Mediterranean Sea, worry free, spreading the Good News. They trusted in Jesus in all their actions. They demonstrated phenomenal courage, as nearly all of them were martyred for their efforts. They utilized prayer for guidance to manage the many issues they had to address. They prayed to God to tell them who was to replace the apostle Judas (Acts 1:21-26); they prayed for the Samaritans to receive the Holy Spirit (Acts 8:14-17); and they prayed for Peter after he was arrested by King Herod (Acts 12:1-5). Divine peace was a hallmark of their lives in all these efforts.

The world today is a culture bound in a state of fear, stress, anxiety, and worry based on worldly and personal issues. Will the pandemic resolve? Are the governments of Russia, China, and North Korea going to plunge us into World War III? Will our economy recover from high inflation? And will our politicians work together, seeking the best interests of all our citizens? We have personal concerns as well. Will I be able to keep my job to support my family? Are our children getting the proper education they need for their futures? Can I get the quality medical treatment needed for a disease? And how can we end family strife?

Each one of us has a choice to make in facing these kinds of worldly and personal challenges. Are we going to rely upon ourselves and let our hearts be troubled and overtaken by fear, stress, anxiety, and worry? Or are we going to follow the four-step process given to us by Our Lord as described above to resolve the issue(s) and live in a state of peace? So many of us let pride get in the way and try to manage the challenge on our own—only to fail and fall into a state of misery.

Following the process given to us by Our Lord to attain peace in our souls yields spiritual bliss. This means to live in a continuous state of joy, happiness, and contentment, doing the will of Jesus. We will further experience grace from God and divine favor for all of our actions. St. Peter confirms this message: "The God of grace who called you to his eternal glory through Christ [Jesus] will himself restore, confirm, strengthen, and establish you after you have suffered a little" (1 Pet. 5:10).

St. Francis of Assisi is the patron saint of peace. He recognized that peace is never simply a human achievement. The only source of it is God. He promoted it among all people, especially for his friars, the Order of St. Clare (the Poor Clares), and the secular Franciscans. He wanted people to experience harmony, which was as fragile in his time as it is today. This saint was an artisan of peace. On October 27, 1986, Pope St. John Paul II invited all religious leaders from around the world to Assisi, Italy, to pray and fast for world peace. The pope called on everyone to be artisans of peace.[15]

St. Paul sums up the issues and remedies for managing fear, stress, anxiety, and worry when he wrote, "No trial has come to you but what is human. God is faithful and will not let you be tried beyond your strength; but with the trial He will also provide a way out, so that you may be able to bear it" (1 Cor. 10:13).

Fear, stress, anxiety, and worry have been around since they were created by Adam and Eve. Down through the millennia and centuries, these symptoms have plagued men and women because we make the choice to allow them to consume our lives. Jesus gives us the remedy for divine peace by following His formula. It is we

---

[15] Pat McCloskey, O.F.M., "St. Francis and His Artisans of Peace," Franciscan Media, May 10, 2020, https://www.franciscanmedia.org /franciscan-spirit-blog/st-francis-and-his-artisans-of-peace/.

who have the opportunity to be artisans of peace and live in a state of contentment doing his will.

> **Spiritual Treasures for Reflection**
>
> Peace I leave with you; my peace I give to you. Not as the world gives do I give it to you. Do not let your hearts be troubled or afraid. (John 14:27)
>
> Have no anxiety at all, but in everything, by prayer and petition, with thanksgiving, make your requests known to God. Then the peace of God that surpasses all understanding will guard your hearts and minds in Christ Jesus. (Phil. 4:6–7)
>
> No trial has come to you but what is human. God is faithful and will not let you be tried beyond your strength, but with the trial He will also provide a way out, so that you may be able to bear it. (1 Cor. 10:13)

Replace Spiritual Mediocrity with Spiritual Maturity

Grace from God: Becoming one of Our Lord's true holy ones

When I was in my early thirties, I was struggling with all kinds of challenges that made me miserable. I was in over my head in my law practice, my father was in poor health, and my wife, Rosalyn, and I were raising three young boys. I was always pressed for time. Joy and happiness were gone from my life. I prayed to Jesus for help. He put the power of the Holy Spirit at work in my soul. He inspired me to outline the New Testament and to improve my prayer life. After only a few days of making this effort, the gifts and fruits of the Holy Spirit came into my soul, ending my misery. Joy and happiness were at work in my life in a way that I never knew before. The Holy Spirit was a spiritual game-changer for me.

Over the next two years, the Holy Spirit inspired me to continue to outline the New Testament. He has been at work in my soul ever since, especially for the challenging times of the passing of my mother and father, a month-long trial in which I defended a company from a hundred-million-dollar lawsuit that would impact four hundred jobs, the cancer diagnosis and treatment of one of our sons, and some personal health problems. The Holy Spirit was there for me during the joyful times as well—for the graduation of our sons from college and grad school, the marriage of our oldest son, Blake, to Ashley, the birth of our grandchildren, Evan and Clare, and the fortieth anniversary of my marriage to Rosalyn.

Please don't let another day pass without activating the Holy Spirit in your life. God sent Him to operate in every soul so we can do His will, maximize the joy in life, and replace spiritual mediocrity with spiritual maturity, living in a state of holiness.

Who is the Holy Spirit? He is the third member of the Holy Trinity, the other two being God the Father and Our Lord Jesus Christ. Jesus called Him the Paraclete, the Advocate, the Consoler, and the Spirit of Truth (CCC 692). Our bodies are temples of the Holy Spirit; He lives in us (1 Cor. 6:19; John 14:17). Our lives are to be governed by the Spirit and not by the flesh (Rom. 8:5).

As described in the Old Testament, the Holy Spirit was at work before Jesus came into the world as our Savior. The prophet Ezekiel writes about God's way of regenerating the people of the time: "I will put my spirit within you so that you walk in my statutes, observe my ordinances, and keep them" (36:27). The prophet Micah further writes about the Spirit at work in him: "But as for me, I am filled with power, with the spirit of the LORD, with justice and with might" (3:8).

The New Testament is filled with numerous phenomenal stories about the power of this third member of the Trinity. Luke's Gospel records that the Holy Spirit initiated the conception of Jesus in Mary (Luke 1:30-35). Thereafter, Mary visited her cousin Elizabeth, who was inspired by the Holy Spirit and cried out in a loud voice, "Most blessed are you among women, and blessed is the fruit of your womb" (Luke 1:42).

At the Last Supper, before Jesus was crucified, He told the apostles that He would send the Holy Spirit to them. He said, "But I tell you the truth, it is better for you that I go. For if I do not go, the Advocate will not come to you. But if I go, I will send him to you.... When he comes, the Spirit of truth, he will guide you to all truth" (John 16:7, 13). Jesus further said, "He will teach you everything and remind you of all that [I] told you" (John 14:26). On the night of His Resurrection, Jesus kept His promise to the apostles, sending the Holy Spirit to them in the upper room. Jesus breathed on the apostles and said, "Receive the holy Spirit" (John 20:22).

Several apostles wrote about the great power of the Holy Spirit:

+ St. Peter wrote, "If you are insulted for the name of Christ, blessed are you, for the Spirit of glory and of God rests upon you" (1 Pet. 4:14).

+ St. Luke wrote about the appearance of the apostles before the Sanhedrin, where they said, "We must obey God rather than men.... We are witnesses of these things, as is the holy Spirit that God has given to those who obey him" (Acts 5:29, 32).

+ St. Paul wrote, "Now to him who is able to accomplish far more than all we ask or imagine, by the power at work within us" (Eph. 3:20).

+ St. Paul further wrote, "For God did not give us a spirit of cowardice but rather of power and love and self-control" (2 Tim. 1:7).

In the book *The Sanctifier*, Archbishop Luis María Martínez of Mexico City tells us about the Spirit of truth. He wrote, "The Holy Spirit frequently speaks to souls, breathes upon them, and inspires them. But they do not hear Him except in the measure of their love for Him. One of the characteristics of love for the

Holy Spirit is solicitous attention to the sound of His voice, to His inspirations."

When the Holy Spirit is active in our souls, He provides us very special gifts and fruits. The gifts are wisdom, understanding, counsel, fortitude, knowledge, piety, and fear of the Lord (see Isa. 11:2). The fruits He gives us are love, joy, peace, patience, kindness, generosity, faithfulness, gentleness, and self-control (Gal. 5:22-23).

Down through the ages—as recorded in the Old and New Testaments, the writings of the saints, the encyclicals of popes, and the books authored by holy ones—there are countless stories of the great power of the Advocate at work in their souls. So, why not for each of us? Don't let another day go by without activating in your soul this third member of the Trinity to maximize the joy in your life.

Many have already experienced the power of the Holy Spirit. During the Sacrament of Baptism, each soul receives the Holy Spirit when anointed with sacred chrism (CCC 1241). In the Sacrament of Confirmation, the bishop, through the grace of God, confers on the soul the gifts of the Holy Spirit, completing the grace of Baptism by the laying on of hands (CCC 1288).

How do we activate the Holy Spirit, Who is present in our souls through these sacraments, to live a spiritually mature life? The answer is very simple. We have to be in union with God, always doing His will through daily prayer, good works, and spiritual growth.

Quality prayer time is easy to do. When you wake up in the morning, pray for guidance from the Holy Spirit to do the will of God in all your thoughts, words, and actions of the day. During the commute to work, pray for your family members and friends who are deceased or are facing challenges in their lives. At lunchtime, reflect on your morning actions and plan your afternoon, seeking direction from the Advocate. In the midafternoon, pause for a few minutes and pray a decade of the Rosary. At the end of the workday, ponder how you were blessed by God in your daily actions, examine your conscience, acknowledge your sins to God, ask for forgiveness, and seek His plan for you for the next day. At dinner, pray with your family. Before bedtime, finish your day with some spiritual reading from the Bible, from a book about one of the saints or from a spiritual author. This type of prayer life keeps a soul focused on the will of God and away from any kind of temptation.

Doing good works each day comes easy to us when the Spirit of truth is at work in our lives. Boredom, worry, and stress cease and are replaced by awesome joy. Good works include taking care of our families, doing our jobs to the best of our ability, helping others in the work place or neighbors, doing house chores, and participating in church ministry or community activities.

The Holy Spirit is there for us in all of the decisions we have to make, whether simple or complex. We get the gifts of wisdom, understanding, and knowledge in deciding small matters, such as the food we choose to nourish our bodies with or the clothes we wear. Most importantly, these same gifts are there for us for difficult decisions, such as who to marry, where to live, the job to work, and health issues. And we receive the gift of courage to execute these decisions.

St. James writes that this special joy from the Holy Spirit is there for us when we face our most challenging times in life. He states, "Consider it all joy, my brothers, when you encounter various trials, for you know that the testing of your faith produces perseverance. And let perseverance be perfect, so that you may be perfect and complete, lacking in nothing" (James 1:2-4).

Spiritual growth is the third requirement to maximize our joy in life through the power of the Holy Spirit at work in our souls.

For most of us, spiritual development has been limited since we left formal religious education in school. Therefore, it is critical that we engage in continuing our spiritual education. This includes spiritual reading from the Bible, the saints, and other spiritual authors. Additionally, we should participate in some type of church ministry or community activity, even if it is limited to only a few hours each month. There are numerous ministry opportunities in our parishes. Bringing the Eucharist to the homebound or nursing homes, serving meals at a homeless shelter, teaching students in the parish school of religion, serving at Mass as a lector or Eucharistic minister, and helping in parish operations are just a few of the endless possibilities for ministry work.

The greatest blessing from allowing the Holy Spirit to be active, operating in our souls every day, is to reach spiritual maturity and live in a state of holiness. There are different types of maturity in the world, such as physical, mental, emotional, social, and spiritual. We reach a state of spiritual holiness when doing the will of Jesus in every situation is automatic, no matter how difficult the demands may be. Jesus tells us to "be perfect, just as your heavenly Father is perfect" (Matt. 5:48).

There are very few guarantees in life. One of them is to reach spiritual maturity. This is accomplished by activating the power of the Holy Spirit at work in us through daily prayer, good works, and spiritual growth. Once a soul has this experience, there are no earthly desires that can match it. So, please make the choice of putting this great power at work in your soul, and become one of Our Lord's holy ones.

Spiritual Treasures for Reflection

I will put my spirit within you so that you walk in my statutes, observe my ordinances, and keep them. (Ezek. 36:27)

[The holy Spirit] will teach you everything and remind you of all that [I] told you. (John 14:26)

For God did not give us a spirit of cowardice but rather of power and love and self-control. (2 Tim. 1:7)

Teaching #8

Be a Catalyst for Jesus: Teach Others His Values to Help Them Reach Heaven

---

Grace from God: Igniting a spiritual fire in others

A *catalyst* is defined by Merriam-Webster as any person or thing that provokes significant change or action. In our lifetime, there have been many things that have been a catalyst for change in the way we live. One of them is the invention of the cell phone, which alters how we communicate with others, access information, and take photographs. Another catalyst is the alternative sources of energy being used in our world today. There is solar, wind, hydroelectric, geothermal, and biomass energy.

In the history of the world, Jesus Christ was the greatest catalyst for spiritual change. He set the world on fire with His focus on spiritual values and not earthly ways. He desperately wanted His teachings to reach all souls so they could reach Heaven. He told His disciples that His purpose on earth was to spread the Good News to others as an example for them to follow. He said, "To the other towns also I must proclaim the good news of the kingdom of God, because for this purpose I have been sent" (Luke 4:43).

As Our Lord was coming to the end of His three years of public ministry, He sent seventy-two of His disciples in pairs to spread the Good News of His teachings to others to help them get to Heaven. The purpose of the disciples in this effort was to be catalysts, to ignite a fire in all those they visited, and to convert them to follow the teachings of Jesus. He specifically said to His disciples, "The harvest is abundant but the laborers are few; so ask the master of the harvest to send out laborers for his harvest" (Luke 10:2).

Even after Jesus was crucified and rose from the dead, He appeared to the disciples and commanded them again to be catalysts to inspire all souls to follow His ways. He said to them, "Go into the whole world and proclaim the gospel to every creature" (Mark 16:15). And the apostles obeyed the command of Jesus: "For so the Lord has commanded us, 'I have made you a light to the Gentiles, that you may be an instrument of salvation to the ends of the earth'" (Acts 13:47). These men spent the rest of their lives spreading the Good News. Jesus warned them that their efforts would not be easy. He said, "Go on your way; behold, I am sending you like lambs among wolves" (Luke 10:3).

The apostles endured many trials and challenges as they traveled to spread the Good News. They baptized thousands of souls and started the Catholic Church from scratch. Some of them were imprisoned for their efforts. Almost all of them were martyred, and all but Judas are saints.

Before God sent Jesus as the Messiah into the world, He directed the prophets to spread the Good News to the people of their time. The prophet Isaiah wrote:

> The spirit of the Lord is upon me,
> because the Lord has anointed me;
> He has sent me to bring good news to the afflicted,

to bind up the brokenhearted,
To proclaim liberty to the captives,
release to the prisoners. (Isa. 61:1)

The prophet Amos was asked by God to do likewise. He wrote, "The LORD took me from following the flock, and the LORD said to me, 'Go, prophesy to my people Israel'" (Amos 7:15).

Our Blessed Mother Mary encourages us to follow this commandment from her Son. Shortly after Our Lady committed to God to be the Mother of Jesus, she visited her cousin Elizabeth in the town of Judah. Elizabeth told Mary, "Most blessed are you among women, and blessed is the fruit of your womb." Mary's response to her was: "My soul proclaims the greatness of the Lord; my spirit rejoices in God my Savior" (Luke 1:42, 46-47). Our spiritual Mother Mary wants us to proclaim the greatness of the Lord to others.

Many saints served as catalysts to ignite a spiritual fire in the people of their time, spreading the Good News to them. In 1540, St. Francis Xavier, a Jesuit priest, was asked by St. Ignatius of Loyola to do missionary work in India and the Far East. He accepted this offer and spent the next twelve years spreading the Good News of Christianity to Portuguese settlements and then in Japan and China. He faced many challenges in his work from local religious and imperial rulers, and sometimes threats of death. St. Francis worked hard to learn the language and culture of those he met within the countries where he worked. He died in 1552 on Shangchuan Island in China.[16]

[16] Krista Stevens, "St. Francis Xavier—Living the Good News of Christ in the Twenty-First Century," Daily Theology, December 3, 2016, https://dailytheology.org/2016/12/03/st-francis-xavier-living-the-good-news-of-christ-in-the-twenty-first-century/.

Spiritual Lightning

In 1840, St. Mother Théodore Guérin and five sister companions from the religious order Sisters of Providence traveled from France to the wilderness of southern Indiana to start a mission to teach the values of Jesus and educate the pioneer children there. Sr. Théodore faced many challenges in these efforts, as the sisters had no place to stay when they arrived, had very little money, did not speak English, nor knew the local customs, and they had to start a school from scratch. She experienced many health issues during her fifteen years of missionary work. Through her efforts, many schools were established, two orphanages were opened, and free pharmacies were founded in southern Indiana.[17]

St. Teresa of Ávila wrote a prayer inspiring all of us to take action to follow the command of Jesus:

Christ has no body now but yours. No hands, no feet on earth but yours. Yours are the eyes through which He looks compassion on the world. Yours are the feet with which He walks to do good. Yours are the hands through which He blesses all the world. Yours are the hands, yours are the feet, yours are the eyes, you are His body. Christ has no body now on earth but yours.[18]

This command to be catalysts for others continues to this day—for all of us. Our Lord tells us to shout His Good News from the housetops: "What I say to you in the darkness, speak in the light; what you hear whispered, proclaim on the housetops" (Matt. 10:27). Being Catholic isn't a spectator sport where we sit

---

[17] "St. Mother Theodore Guerin's Story," Sisters of Providence of Saint Mary-of-the-Woods, https://spsmw.org/about/saint-mother -theodore-guerin/her-story/.

[18] The Collected Works of St. Teresa of Avila.

on the sidelines and watch others fulfill this commandment. Each one of us has a calling to evangelize others. We owe it to Jesus to accept this responsibility in thanksgiving for all of the blessings He has bestowed on us.

The idea of fulfilling this commandment may cause us to experience doubt about working for Him. But Our Lord encourages us to stand up for our beliefs and not to worry, telling us, "Do not worry how you are to speak or what you are to say. You will be given at that moment what you are to say. For it will not be you who speak but the Spirit of your Father speaking through you" (Matt. 10:19–20).

In the summer of 2015, Ashley Code, a high school student at Mount Carmel Academy in New Orleans, was diagnosed with an inoperable brain tumor. Over the course of the next year, she underwent intense treatment for the tumor, including radiation and chemotherapy. During this time, she didn't blame Jesus or lose her faith. Instead, she used this time to spread the Good News to her teachers, classmates, friends, and family members. One of her favorite expressions was "Be the face of Jesus to others." Sadly, Ashley passed away on September 1, 2016.

Spreading the Good News begins at home, in our families. Parents have the duty to raise their children in the practice of the Faith, teaching them the values of Jesus. Spouses have the duty to treat one another just as Jesus would. It is the primary duty of parents to do all that they can to help their children get to Heaven and for spouses to do likewise for one another.

Proclaiming the Good News extends beyond our families and to everyone with whom we communicate. This includes conversations with our work colleagues, store clerks, educators, students, neighbors, those in ministry, and all others. These communications can be in the form of e-mails, texts, tweets, Instagram posts, and general conversation. Every one of our communications has to be based on core Christian values.

Don't be afraid to stand up to others in conversation about your beliefs as to the right to life, receiving the Body of Christ in the Eucharist at Mass, the other sacraments, daily prayer, or the teachings of the Church. Similarly, have no fear in challenging others in their cultural beliefs that are counter to the teachings of Jesus. St. Paul wrote, "Say these things. Exhort and correct with all authority. Let no one look down on you" (Titus 2:15).

Think about it this way. Can we really expect to be a positive influence on others if we are not carrying the torch for Our Lord? Our suffering and searching brothers and sisters must be shown the sheer goodness of God by our conduct to have a real chance of opening their hearts to Our Lord's ways. We have to remember that it has been said it takes years to build a trust relationship with others but only one bad act or comment to destroy this relationship.

We can spread Our Lord's ways by doing small things in service to others. Consider donating an hour or two of your time to help a disabled neighbor, a coworker who needs assistance on a project, visit a sick friend or family member, or write a note to someone who needs encouragement. Pray for those who are suffering in your daily prayers. These small acts are a witness to Jesus at work in us, and others will want to do the same.

Our church parishes have numerous ministry opportunities as well. We can bring the Eucharist to the homebound or to those in nursing homes and hospitals, cook and serve meals at homeless shelters, volunteer with the Knights of Columbus or the St. Vincent de Paul Society to help the poor, teach religious education to children on Sunday mornings, or do administrative work in the parish office. The joy of doing ministry work to help others is awesome.

The response to our efforts to spread the Good News will likely be mixed. Some will ignore or criticize you for your efforts, but know that you are planting seeds in their souls which will be harvested later. Others will be lukewarm in their response. For some, you will help them to grow closer to Our Lord. Don't ever get discouraged in your actions nor let any criticism dull your enthusiasm to spread the Good News.

Pope St. John XXIII wrote an encyclical which sums up the call from Our Lord. In *Peace on Earth*, this saint wrote: "Every believer in this world of ours must be a spark of light, the center of love, a vivifying leaven amongst his fellow men."[19] Mother Angelica further explains that, "this world is never going to see the Good News by reading the good book. Because they won't read it. They are only going to see it when you live it."[20]

At the end of Mass, the priest gives a final blessing. Then he says, "Go and announce the Gospel of the Lord." This expression is said hundreds of thousands of times every day in Masses around the world. Are we listening to this call to be catalysts for Jesus, spreading His teachings to help others get to Heaven?

---

[19] Pope St. John XXIII, encyclical Pacem in Terris (April 11, 1963), no. 164.

[20] Arroyo, *Mother Angelica's Little Book*,.

Spiritual Treasures for Reflection

The harvest is abundant but the laborers are few; so ask the master of the harvest to send out laborers for his harvest. (Luke 10:2)

For so the Lord has commanded us, "I have made you a light to the Gentiles, that you may be an instrument of salvation to the ends of the earth." (Acts 13:47)

This world is never going to see the Good News by reading the good book. Because they won't read it. They are only going to see it when you live it. (Mother Angelica)

Teaching #9

The Eucharist and Confession Are the Highways to Heaven

Sacrament of the Eucharist

Grace from God: The Sacrament of the Eucharist
is the bread of the strong that gives us the strength to
perform the mission Jesus calls us to do each day

In recent times, nearly all health experts promote various food supplements and diets for us to live a long life. Many of these experts advocate for different exercise programs as a further key to a quality life. There are seemingly countless television commercials, phone apps, YouTube videos, and social media ads that bombard us with these messages. It is estimated that consumers worldwide spend over 96 billion dollars annually on these food products and services and over 264 billion on fitness programs and equipment. All of this money and effort can only add so many years to our earthly lives. As of 2024, the oldest living person is 117 years of age. Eventually, all of us pass from this life.

Spiritual Lightning

It is critical to recognize that a healthy spiritual life has infinitely more value. It prepares us for eternity in Heaven rather than simply adding to our limited time here on earth through healthy, physical bodies. Our spiritual experts Jesus Christ, His Blessed Mother Mary, the saints, and our Church all advocate that frequent consumption of the Eucharist and regular Confession are essential for a healthy spiritual life that will lead us to a most joyful life and eternity in Heaven. Imagine if the eight billion souls in the world today focused the same amount of time and effort on a healthy spiritual life as is being spent on healthy, earthly activities. Our world would be less like Hell on earth and more like Heaven on earth. It is important to recognize that the Sacraments of the Eucharist and Confession are free—they cost nothing. These two sacraments are available every day and are essential for a joyful, healthy spiritual life and eternity in Heaven.

During Our Lord's public ministry, He performed the miracle of the multiplication of loaves and fishes to feed five thousand people. The next day, He crossed the Sea of Galilee to Capernaum and preached to the crowds about the importance of the Eucharist, saying,

> I am the living bread that came down from heaven; whoever eats this bread will live forever; and the bread that I will give is my flesh for the life of the world.... Amen, amen I say to you, unless you eat the flesh of the Son of Man and drink his blood, you do not have life within you. Whoever eats my flesh and drinks my blood has eternal life, and I will raise him on the last day. For my flesh is true food, and my blood is true drink. Whoever eats my flesh and drinks my blood remains in me and I in him.... This is the bread that came down from heaven. Unlike your ancestors who

ate and still died, whoever eats this bread will live forever. (John 6:51, 53–56, 58)

At the Last Supper, Jesus further spoke about the importance of partaking of the Eucharist. This dinner has been designated as the Institution of the Eucharist. The night before His Passion and Crucifixion, Jesus gave the apostles instructions to follow on their mission: "Then he took the bread, said the blessing, broke it, and gave it to them, saying, 'This is my body, which will be given for you; do this in memory of me.' And likewise the cup after they had eaten, saying, 'This cup is the new covenant in my blood, which will be shed for you'" (Luke 22:19–20).

In every Mass, our Catholic Church commemorates the words Jesus spoke during His public ministry and at the Last Supper. These words are said hundreds of thousands of times every day by more than four hundred thousand Catholic priests who celebrate Mass. This is a testimonial to the efforts of the Church to carry out the instructions from Jesus to make the Eucharist available every day to all souls.

Our Blessed Mother, Mary, appeared to three children in Fátima, Portugal, in May of 1917. They were Lúcia dos Santos, Francisco Marto, and Jacinta Marto. Her appearance is rooted in the Eucharist. Before Our Lady's apparition, there were three visits to these children by the Angel of Peace. His visits discussed the veneration of the Eucharist and the consumption of Holy Communion. In Our Lady's first apparition, she showed the children a light so bright that they created a prayer referring to the Eucharist and the Trinity. The prayer states, "O most Holy Trinity, I adore You! My God, my God, I love You in the most Blessed Sacrament."[21]

---

[21] Dr. Richard Nicholas, "The Significance of the Eucharist in the Apparitions of Fatima," *Homiletic and Pastoral Review*, December

There are those who question whether the Eucharist is truly the *Real* Presence of Jesus. The amount of proof in support of the conversion of the bread and wine into the Body and Blood of Jesus is exhaustive. It is the action of the Holy Spirit that brings about this transubstantiation.

St. Ambrose wrote about this conversion. "Be convinced that this is not what nature has formed, but what the blessing has consecrated. The power of the blessing prevails over that of nature, because by the blessing nature itself is changed.... Could not Christ's word, which can make from nothing what did not exist, change existing things into what they were not before? It is no less a feat to give things their original nature than to change their nature" (CCC 1375, quoting *De myst.* 9,50; 52).

Down through the centuries, there have been many miracles as further proof that the Eucharist is truly the Body and Blood of Jesus. The Church has recognized more than one hundred of them. Here are a few representative samples.

In 1263, a German priest was celebrating Mass in Bolsena, Italy. Shortly after the Consecration, the Host began to bleed. After investigating the bloody Host and the bloodstained corporal, Pope Urban IV declared it authentic. It was from this miracle that the Feast of Corpus Christi originated.

In the eighth century in Lanciano, Italy, a priest was saying the prayer of consecration at Mass when he saw the bread and wine converted into human flesh and blood. An investigation in 1971 by a professor of anatomy, Edoardo Linoli, revealed that it was human cardiac tissue. The flesh and blood are preserved in an exhibit in the Church of San Francisco in Lanciano.

12, 2017, https://www.hprweb.com/2017/12/the-significance-of-the-eucharist-in-the-apparitions-at-fatima/.

In 2008, two priests and a religious sister were distributing Communion during Mass in Mexico. One of the Hosts that the religious sister held began to effuse a reddish substance. The local bishop asked Dr. Ricardo Gomez and his team to conduct scientific research on it. In 2013, the team concluded that the reddish substance corresponds to blood in which there is DNA of human origin. The blood type is the same as the one found in the Host of Lanciano.

Blessed Carlo Acutis passed away at age fifteen in 2006 from leukemia. He created a website dedicated to listing every reported Eucharistic miracle. He spent four years in this effort. He was a very holy young man who found strength in the Eucharist. He said, "The more Eucharist we receive, the more we will become like Jesus, so that on earth we will have a foretaste of heaven." He further said that "the Eucharist is the Highway to Heaven."[22]"

In further support of the importance of this sacrament as spiritual nourishment for our souls, Jesus has given many private revelations. One of them was to St. Maria Faustina Kowalska. She wrote in her diary about her many private apparitions of Jesus and our Blessed Mother. In one of her entries, she describes the importance of receiving the Eucharist daily: "Every morning during meditation, I prepare myself for the whole day's struggle. Holy Communion assures me that I will win the victory; and so it is. I fear the day when I do not receive Holy Communion. This Bread of the strong gives me all the strength I need to carry on my mission and the courage to do whatever the Lord asks of me."[23]

---

[22] Aaron Lambert, "Highway to Heaven: Learning from Carlo Acutis's Eucharistic Fervor," *Denver Catholic*, November 17, 2022, https://denvercatholic.org/highway-to-heaven-learning-from-carlo-acutiss-eucharistic-fervor/.

[23] *Diary of St. Maria Faustina Kowalska: Divine Mercy in My Soul* [hereafter *Diary*] (Stockbridge, MA: Marain Press, 2005), no. 91.

Spiritual Lightning

The effects of the Eucharist on our souls are plentiful. The Eucharist preserves, increases, and renews the life of grace that we received at Baptism. It helps preserve us from future temptation and sin. The Eucharist is the food of eternal life. By sharing in the Body and Blood of our Savior, we are drawn into communion with Him. We participate with the whole community in Our Lord's sacrifice. This sacrament is the source and summit of our Christian lives (CCC 1392, 1395, 1212, 790, 1322, and 1324).

Eucharistic Adoration is a phenomenal way to spend time alone with Jesus, whether in front of a closed tabernacle or in the presence of the exposed Host in a monstrance. In Adoration, we acknowledge that we are simply creatures exalting the greatness of the Lord Who made us. We pay homage to the Spirit of the King of Glory. It is our opportunity to be one-on-one with Our Lord, to speak to Him about anything we have on our minds, to offer prayers for others, to thank Him for His many blessings to us, and to be at total peace (CCC 2628, 2096).

Sometimes I think about the joyful times of raising our three sons, Blake, Kyle, and Grant. Our family has been blessed with so many wonderful experiences. The day of each of their First Communions was truly exceptional. The joy on their faces from receiving the Eucharist for the first time was awesome.

We have a choice each week of how we spend our time. Much of it is committed to raising our families and to our jobs. But we all have some discretionary time to spend on activities we enjoy, whether it be exercising our bodies, sports, social media, or being with friends. These outside activities only give us temporary earthly joy. Let us consider spending some time exercising our souls in attending Mass, in partaking of the Eucharist, or in Adoration time, one-on-one with our Creator, Who gave us life. The greatest joy in any weekly activity we choose comes from partaking in these spiritual acts.

Scott Hahn is a former Presbyterian minister who converted to Catholicism. He has a PhD in systematic theology from Marquette University, is the author of many books, and currently teaches at Franciscan University. Early in his career, he served as pastor at Trinity Presbyterian Church in Fairfax, Virginia. Curiosity about the Catholic Faith drove him to his first Mass in a chapel in Milwaukee, Wisconsin. Up to this point in time, he thought of the Eucharist as a human sacrilege. During this first Mass, he thought of all of the Scripture references to Isaiah, St. Paul, and the Psalms. He heard the priest say, "This is my Body.... This is the cup of my Blood." At that point, a prayer surged in his heart: "My Lord and my God, that's really You." He converted to Catholicism on Easter in 1986.[24]

The Eucharist can be described as a glimpse of Heaven on earth, commemorating the sacrifice of Our Lord's Passion and Crucifixion. It helps light up our journey on earth to fulfill the will of God in our daily endeavors. It keeps us strong and resistant to the temptations from the evil one. All who partake of the Eucharist experience a healthy spiritual life on our way to eternity in Heaven.

Sacrament of Confession

---

*Grace from God: Confession washes away sins
and restores happiness to our souls*

When our three sons were living with us at home, sometimes we would be in a time jam trying to get to an event. On one of these occasions, I could not find my car keys. I was searching around

---

[24] Scott Hahn, *The Lamb's Supper: The Mass as Heaven on Earth* (New York: Doubleday, 1999), 8.

the house, urgently looking for them. Getting pretty desperate, I began praying to St. Anthony for help. My son Kyle asked me what I was looking for. I told him that I lost my car keys. He looked at me with this quirky facial expression and said, "Dad, I think they are in your pocket." In response, I stared at him, realizing that the lost keys *were* in my pocket, and laughed at myself.

Sometimes we can feel lost in our lives due to sins we commit. Joy and peace are missing from our souls when we engage in sinful conduct. We are searching for a solution to this misconduct. The only remedy for these sins is to seek forgiveness from Our Lord through the Sacrament of Confession. Partaking of this sacrament will end that feeling of being lost and restore true happiness in our hearts.

There are all kinds of sins we can commit. They include pride, anger, gluttony, lust, envy, greed, and laziness. The Ten Commandments address the sins of idolatry, misusing the Lord's name, adultery, theft, murder, bearing false witness against others, and coveting a neighbor's property (Exod. 20:1–17). St. Paul describes additional sins that offend Our Lord, such as wickedness, evil, malice, rivalry, treachery, spite, and scandalmongering (Rom. 1:29–30). Being human and living in a world that often promotes misconduct, we can fall prey to these temptations and transgressions.

Our Lord and Savior Jesus came into the world to save us all from our sinfulness by His death on the Cross. He is described as the Physician of our souls (CCC 1421). He wants us to be reconciled with His Father so we can reach eternal salvation.

In Luke's Gospel, Jesus teaches us about His mercy by forgiving a woman of her sins. While Our Lord was in the house of a Pharisee for dinner, a woman began to wash His feet with her tears. Then she wiped His feet, kissed them, and anointed them.

Jesus offered forgiveness to the woman for her sins, saying, "So I tell you, her many sins have been forgiven; hence, she has shown great love" (Luke 7:47).

Jesus instituted the Sacrament of Confession, or Reconciliation, on the night of His Resurrection when He appeared to the apostles in the Upper Room. He gave them the power to forgive sins. He told them, "Receive the holy Spirit. Whose sins you forgive are forgiven them, and whose sins you retain are retained" (John 20:22–23).

Through the Sacrament of Holy Orders, priests are given the power from Our Lord to forgive sins. They utilize this power through the Sacrament of Confession, also known as Reconciliation.

There are several steps to follow in order to properly engage in this sacrament. First, you must examine your conscience, identifying sins you have committed since your last confession. Then you must be sorry for your sins. Next, you must have a firm resolve to avoid the sins in the future. Thereafter, you see the priest who will greet you with the Sign of the Cross, confess your sins to him. Be straightforward as you state them. Through the power of Jesus, the priest will forgive you of your sins. The priest may offer you some advice to help you avoid these transgressions in the future. Next, the priest will give you penance, which usually is a few prayers, a Scripture reading, a fast of some kind, or an act of charity. Finally, he will ask you to say the Act of Contrition. In closing the sacrament, the priest will give you a blessing, telling you that the Lord has forgiven your sins and to go in peace.

This sacrament only takes about ten to fifteen minutes of your time. The great joy that comes from a good confession is superior to any temporary happiness that comes from any kind of sinful misconduct. We experience divine grace when we partake of this sacrament. Our souls have been washed from their iniquities and cleansed as white as snow. Our Lord pardons all our sins, heals all our ills, redeems us from the pit, and crowns us with mercy and compassion (see Ps. 103:3–4).

Consider participating in the Sacrament of Confession on a monthly basis, as it will result in a true conversion of our souls. As we regularly examine our conscience, this often reveals repetition of the same sinful misconduct. It becomes embarrassing to confess the same sins over and over again, which will help us with the self-discipline we need to avoid them in the future. The grace of Jesus will help us resolve these repetitive sins, thereby restoring joy and peace to our hearts.

Our Lord tells us in the Gospel of Luke about the great joy that happens when one sinner repents for misconduct. He says, "There will be more joy in heaven over one sinner who repents than over ninety-nine righteous people who have no need of repentance.... I tell you, there will be rejoicing among the angels of God over one sinner who repents" (Luke 15:7, 10).

Jesus never gives up on us. His patience never wears thin. He is anxiously waiting for all souls to return to Him. The Son of God is our Good Shepherd. He has an enormous heart. The Sacrament of Confession is a spiritual difference-maker that is essential for a joyful, healthy spiritual life and for eternal life in Heaven. Even if you haven't participated in the sacrament in many years, just go!

Spiritual Treasures for Reflection

This is my body, which will be given for you; do this in memory of me.... This cup is the new covenant in my blood, which will be shed for you. (Luke 22:19-20)

O most Holy Trinity, I adore You! My God, my God, I love You in the Most Blessed Sacrament. (Fátima seers)

Receive the holy Spirit. Whose sins you forgive are forgiven them, and whose sins you retain are retained. (John 20:22-23)

Teaching #10

Devotion to Our Blessed Mother Mary

Grace from God: Our Lady wraps every soul in her mantle
to help them in their greatest challenges

On May 13, 1981, a world leader was shot four times with a semiautomatic pistol, which should have killed him. Three bullets struck him during the attack. This leader had emergency surgery and survived. The day of this tragedy was the feast day of Our Lady of Fátima. Pope St. John Paul II gave thanks to Our Blessed Mother Mary for interceding with her Son Jesus for a miracle to survive this shooting. A bullet recovered from the scene occupies the middle of the crown atop the statue of Our Lady of Fátima in Portugal. Our Lady was a huge part of the life of this saint.[25]

Many of us fail to recognize the important role that our Blessed Mother Mary has in our lives, which is to draw us closer to Jesus. We tend to put her on the sidelines in our spiritual journey, only

---

[25] Fr. Raymond J. de Souza, "The Saint and the Lady Who Saved Him: John Paul II and Fatima," *National Catholic Register*, May 6, 2017, https://www.ncregister.com/commentaries/the-saint-and -the-lady-who-saved-him-john-paul-ii-and-fatima.

thinking of her on her feast days a few times a year. This is a grave mistake! Our Blessed Mother is the greatest woman who ever lived. Our Lord specifically told us this when He was hanging on the Cross. Jesus told the apostle John, "Behold, your mother" (John 19:27). Our Lady has one goal in mind, which is to help every soul get to Heaven. All of us need to build a strong relationship with her, as she is our principal intercessor with the Sacred Heart of Jesus.

As our spiritual Mother, Mary truly guides us in our journey through this life to reach Heaven. She is our role model to follow by the way she instructed all of us, how she lived her life, as recorded in the Gospels, her Assumption into Heaven, her coronation as Queen of Heaven and Earth, her apparitions around the world, and her intercessory powers to her Son Jesus, resulting in thousands of miracles. Our Lord blessed us with His Mother to be there for us every day, providing us with the graces and blessings that we need in this world.

Mary's calling to be our spiritual Mother, teaching us to say *yes* to the will of Jesus, started when the angel Gabriel appeared to her as a teenage girl living in Nazareth. Gabriel said to her:

> "Hail, favored one! The Lord is with you.... Do not be afraid, Mary, for you have found favor with God. Behold, you will conceive in your womb and bear a son, and you shall name him Jesus.... The holy Spirit will come upon you, and the power of the Most High will overshadow you. Therefore the child to be born will be called holy, the Son of God." Our Blessed Mother responded, saying, "Behold, I am the handmaid of the Lord. May it be done to me according to your word." (Luke 1:28, 30-31, 35, 38).

Our Lady's commitment to do the will of God as the Mother of Jesus was filled with great responsibilities. She was guided by the Holy Spirit to raise Him in the practice of the Faith, to teach Him to avoid the temptations of the world, and to help Him stay focused on the will of God. Perhaps her biggest challenge was to be perfect, living without any stain of sin. She was always there for Jesus: at the presentation in the temple after Jesus was born, finding Him in the temple when He was lost, being with Him along the way in His public ministry, praying at the foot of the Cross during His Crucifixion, gathering in the upper room after Jesus rose from the dead, and watching Him ascend into Heaven.

As our spiritual Mother, Mary tells us directly to do the will of God. She said, "Do whatever he tells you" (John 2:5). She is there for us as we fulfill our commitment to do the will of God. Blessed Mother Mary provides us with the graces and blessings we need in the many roles we are called to in life, such as a student, parent, worker, sibling, neighbor, or friend.

The Mother of Jesus further taught us to help others. After Mary accepted the call to be the Mother of Jesus, she left Nazareth to help her cousin Elizabeth, who was six months pregnant with John the Baptist (Luke 1:36-45). Also, she instructed us to spread the Good News of Jesus to others, saying, "My soul proclaims the greatness of the Lord; my spirit rejoices in God my Savior" (Luke 1:46-47).

Special grace from God was given to Mary to be free of all sin during her life on earth (CCC 411). After her death, her body and soul were taken up to Heaven, and she was exalted by Our Lord as Queen of all things (CCC 966).

Bl. Anne Catherine Emmerich recorded visions of the life of Our Lady. This Blessed was a nun in the Augustinian order in Dülmen, Germany. For twelve years before her death, she bore the stigmata of Our Lord. In one of her recorded entries, Bl. Emmerich wrote about Our Lady's Assumption into Heaven:

In the night I saw several of the apostles and holy women praying and singing in the little garden in front of the rock-tomb. A broad shaft of light came down from heaven to the rock, and I saw descending in it a triple-ringed glory of angels and spirits surrounding the appearance of Our Lord and of the shining soul of Mary.... Then I saw the soul of the Blessed Virgin, which had been following the appearance of Our Lord, pass in front of Him, and float down into the tomb. Soon afterwards I saw her soul, united to her transfigured body, rising out of the tomb far brighter and clearer, and ascending into the heavenly Jerusalem with Our Lord and with the whole glory.[26]

There have been many apparitions of Mary, Queen of Heaven and Earth. They have happened all over the world since her Assumption into Heaven. In 352, she appeared to an elderly couple in Rome, Italy. On an August night, Mary asked the couple for a shrine to be built on the Esquiline Hill. The next morning, the hill was covered with snow. Today, the Church of St. Mary of the Snows stands on top of this site as one of the largest of all churches dedicated to our spiritual Mother. August 5 is the feast day of Our Lady of the Snows. In Belleville, Illinois, Our Lady of the Snows shrine is dedicated to the special role of Our Lady in the Church.[27]

In 1251, Our Lady appeared to the prior general of the Carmelite Order, St. Simon Stock, in Aylesford, England. During the

---

[26] *The Life of the Blessed Virgin Mary from the Visions of Anne Catherine Emmerich*, trans. Sir Michael Palairet, 227, A Catholic Moment, https://www.acatholic.org/wp-content/uploads/2014/05/Life-of-Blessed-Virgin-Mary.pdf.

[27] "About Us," National Shrine of Our Lady of the Snows, https://snows.org/about-us/.

apparition, our Blessed Mother gave him the Brown Scapular to wear. She intended for all souls to wear it as an outward sign of her love for everyone. The scapular consists of two panels of cloth joined together by string and worn over the shoulders. Wearing a scapular demonstrates devotion to Our Blessed Mother and living according to the values of Jesus through Mary, who will help us do so. Those who wear the scapular and live the virtues of Jesus and Mary "shall not suffer the eternal fire," Mary promised.[28]

On December 9, 1531, our Blessed Mother appeared to Juan Diego on Tepeyac Hill in Mexico. She requested that a shrine be built to her on the site of this apparition. The bishop wanted confirmation of this request from her. As a sign for the bishop, the Virgin Mary left an image of herself imprinted on the tilma of Juan Diego. After nearly five hundred years, there are no signs of decay on the tilma, which defies all scientific explanations. A basilica has been constructed there. Twenty-four popes have recognized Our Lady of Guadalupe. Each year, approximately ten million people visit this basilica.[29]

Our Lady has the power to intercede with her Son, Jesus, for specific prayer requests we can make to her (CCC 2677, 2679). The angel Gabriel specifically told Our Lady that her cousin Elizabeth, who was thought to be barren, was six months pregnant and that "nothing will be impossible for God" (Luke 1:36–37). Countless

---

[28] Joseph Pronechen, "Put on Our Lady's Protection with the Brown Scapular," *National Catholic Register*, July 16, 2017, https://www.ncregister.com/features/put-on-our-lady-s-protection-with-the-brown-scapular.

[29] Catholic News Agency, "December 12 – Our Lady of Guadalupe," *Catholic Telegraph*, December 11, 2023, https://www.thecatholictelegraph.com/december-12-our-lady-of-guadalupe/71211

miracles and healings are attributable to the intercessory power of Our Lady with her Son, Jesus.

Perhaps the most prolific place where thousands of healings and miracles have occurred is in Lourdes, France. After Mary's appearance to St. Bernadette in 1858, pilgrims began visiting the grotto and reporting numerous miracles. Today, there are about four million visitors per year to the site. Over seven thousand cures and miracles have been reported.[30]

In December 1965 in South Vietnam, a two-year-old boy was suffering from an advanced stage of malaria. There was no medication available to treat this disease. The treating doctors told his parents that the child would die. The parents went to their Catholic church and began praying for several hours in front of the statue of Our Lady of Fátima, asking our Blessed Mother Mary to intercede to her Son, Jesus, as she was their last hope. Over the next few days, the baby boy began to improve. They took him to the physicians for a follow-up visit and discovered that he was cured of the disease. This baby is now a successful businessman and a parishioner in Holy Name of Mary Parish in Bedford, Virginia.

Mother Angelica is the founder of the EWTN global Catholic television network. For forty-two years, she had been crippled and unable to walk without leg braces and crutches after an injury she suffered working with a floor-buffer machine. On January 27, 1998, an Italian mystic named Paola Albertini visited her at the network. The next night, Mother Angelica and the mystic began praying the Rosary together in her office. During the fourth decade, Ms. Albertini paused and told Mother that she had a message from the

---

[30] Lauren Woodrell, "3 Healing Miracles of Our Lady of Lourdes," Magis Center, February 10, 2023, https://www.magiscenter.com/blog/healing-miracles-of-our-lady-of-lourdes.

Blessed Virgin. Thereafter, as they continued to pray the fourth decade together, Mother had a feeling that God wished to heal her. A few minutes later, the mystic fell to her knees and said a prayer in Italian. Then she asked Mother to remove her braces. After some hesitancy, Mother Angelica was able to walk, as she had not done in forty-two years. This good news spread like wildfire. The next day, crowds gathered at the network to see her miraculous healing.[31]

In 2002, Hurricane Lili passed through Lafayette, Louisiana. Mrs. Albertine Locklear was living in a small house next to a giant cell phone tower. During the storm, she was praying the Rosary in the center of her home. She received a spiritual inspiration to walk to her bedroom on the side of her house to continue in prayer. Within minutes, the cell phone tower crashed through the center of her home where she had been praying. Mrs. Locklear is certain that her life was spared that awful day by the intercession of Our Lady with her Son.

In January 2023, John Petrovich of Pittsburgh, Pennsylvania, was jogging through a neighborhood when he saw an ambulance in the driveway of a home. He prayed a Hail Mary for the patient in the emergency vehicle. A week later, Mr. Petrovich was jogging in front of the same driveway, and a lady stopped him. She told him that he had saved her life. She explained that while she was being transported to the hospital, Jesus appeared to her and held out His hand with the face of Mr. Petrovich depicted in the palm. Jesus told her she was going to die, but the prayer to His Mother saved her life.[32]

---

[31] Glenn Dallaire, "Mother Angelica's Two Miraculous Cures," Mystics of the Church, May 2015, https://www.mysticsofthechurch.com/2015/05/mother-angelicas-two-miraculous-cures.html.

[32] Joseph Pronechen, "The Astonishing Power of One Hail Mary," *National Catholic Register*, March 28, 2023, https://www.ncregister.com/features/the-astonishing-power-of-one-hail-mary.

There are numerous ways to build a relationship with our spiritual Mother so that we can experience her many graces, blessings, and intercessions. The simplest way is through prayer. The faithful take refuge in prayer to the Mother of God in all our perils and needs.[33] The Rosary has been described as the most convenient and fruitful means of obtaining her aid.[34] When we pray to Our Lady, she wraps us in her mantle to help us in our greatest challenges in life.

In 1214, St. Dominic had a vision of Mary where she presented him with the beads and prayers to be said for the Rosary. The saint had a tremendous devotion to Mary and the Rosary and promoted it throughout his travels. Spending time each day praying the Rosary and meditating on the mysteries brings true peace and grace. Several friends of mine say the Rosary at night when they have difficulty sleeping.

Other prayers to Our Lady include the Hail Holy Queen, the Memorare, the Angelus, the Magnificat, and the Chaplet of Divine Mercy.

On December 10, 1925, St. Lúcia dos Santos had a vision of the Blessed Mother Mary in Fátima, Portugal. This event initiated the Devotion to the Immaculate Heart of Mary on the first Saturday of five consecutive months. The devotion consists of going to Confession, receiving Communion, reciting five decades of the Rosary, and meditating for fifteen minutes on the mysteries of the Rosary on the first Saturday of five consecutive months. The confession may be made during the eight days preceding or following the

---

[33] Second Vatican Council, Dogmatic Constitution on the Church *Lumen Gentium* (November 21, 1964), VIII, 66.

[34] Pope Pius XII, encyclical *Ingruentium Malorum* (September 15, 1951), no. 8.

first Saturday of each month, provided that Holy Communion is received in a state of grace. These conditions should be fulfilled with the intention of making reparation for sins against the Immaculate Heart of Mary. By fulfilling these conditions, Our Lady promises to obtain for us, at the hour of our death, the graces necessary for salvation. This devotion was approved by Pope St. Pius X in 1904.[35]

Numerous popes have written encyclicals and other documents dedicated to enhancing the devotion to our Blessed Mother. Pope Leo XIII merits the title "the Pope of the Rosary." Twenty-two of his documents are devoted to the Holy Rosary. Other popes who have written about Mary include Pius V, Pius IX, Pius X, Pius XI, Pius XII, Leo XII, John XIII, Paul XI, and John Paul II.[36]

Solid devotion to our Blessed Mother, Mary, is a must in our spiritual journey through life. To keep her on the sidelines is a grave error of epic proportions. The Queen of Heaven and Earth has only one goal: to help every soul reach Heaven. We can't ignore her instructions to us as recorded in the Gospels, her assumption into heaven, her many apparitions around the world, and her intercessory powers with her Son, Jesus, which have resulted in thousands of miracles. She is the principal intercessor to the Sacred Heart of Jesus. He told her through the angel Gabriel that "nothing will be impossible for God" (Luke 1:37). Our Lady provides us with graces and blessings that we need each day in this life.

---

[35] Fr. John Zuhlsdorf, "Answering Our Lady's Call: Five First Saturdays at St. Mary of Pine Bluff," Roman Catholic Man, May 23, 2017, https://romancatholicman.com/wp/answering-ladys-call-five-first-saturdays-st-mary-pine-bluff/).

[36] George P. Morse, *Précis of Official Catholic Teaching on Marian Devotions*.

Spiritual Treasures for Reflection

Hail, favored one! The Lord is with you.... Do not be afraid, Mary, for you have found favor with God. Behold, you will conceive in your womb and bear a son, and you shall name him Jesus. (Luke 1:28, 30–31)

Nothing will be impossible for God. (Luke 1:37)

Do whatever he tells you. (John 2:5)

Teaching #11

Prayer Time with Jesus Is the Most Important Time of the Day

Grace from God: Developing a mature relationship with Jesus

Demands for our time are more challenging than ever. It seems as if we are on a time treadmill with no way to get off. Most of our day is fixed with time obligations for our jobs, meals, homework with the kids, and housework. Our discretionary time is often tied up with entertaining ourselves with television, the Internet, or social media. There seems to be very little time for Jesus in prayer. This is a mistake!

Our Lord taught us the importance of prayer when He went to the Garden of Gethsemane shortly before He began His Passion and Crucifixion. After the Last Supper, Jesus went to this garden with the apostles to pray to His Father. While there, He asked Peter, James, and John to pray with Him for an hour, but they fell asleep. Jesus was frustrated with them, and He said to Peter, "So you could not keep watch with me for one hour? Watch and pray that you may not undergo the test. The spirit is willing, but the flesh is weak" (Matt. 26:40–41).

Peter and John learned from that night in the garden. An hour of prayer became a regular part of their daily lives. They developed a practice of praying for an hour beginning at 3:00 p.m. (Acts 3:1). Priests and deacons are obligated to spend time in daily prayer as part of their ministry. So why can't the rest of us spend some time every day in prayer too?

Jesus had an awesome relationship with God His Father by a persistent daily prayer life and living an abundant life here on earth. His strong prayer life kept Him focused on doing the will of God always.

The Gospels record Jesus in prayer over twenty times in many different situations as evidence of how important it is to have a strong prayer life. Our Lord desperately wants us to have a strong prayer life too, which helps us build a mature relationship with Him, bringing us constant joy and happiness in doing His will. There are numerous examples of Jesus praying to His Father:

- + *Alone with God:* "Rising very early before dawn, he left and went off to a deserted place, where he prayed" (Mark 1:35; see also Matt. 14:23).
- + *At His baptism:* "After all the people had been baptized and Jesus also had been baptized and was praying, heaven was opened and the holy Spirit descended upon him in bodily form like a dove" (Luke 3:21–22).
- + *In public, to convince others about the importance of prayer:* "So they took away the stone. And Jesus raised his eyes and said, 'Father, I thank you for hearing me. I know that you always hear me; but because of the crowd here I have said this, that they may believe that you sent me'" (John 11:41–42).
- + *Before important decisions:* "In those days he departed to the mountain to pray, and he spent the night in prayer to

God. When day came, he called his disciples to himself, and from them he chose Twelve, whom he also named apostles" (Luke 6:12–13).

+ *Before performing a miracle:* "He took [the deaf man] off by himself away from the crowd. He put his finger into the man's ears and, spitting, touched his tongue; then he looked up to heaven and groaned, and said to him, '*Ephphatha!*' (that is, 'Be opened!') And [immediately] the man's ears were opened, his speech impediment was removed, and he spoke plainly" (Mark 7:33–35).

+ *At the Last Supper:* "Then he took the bread, said the blessing, broke it, and gave it to them, saying, 'This is my body, which will be given for you; do this in memory of me.' And likewise the cup after they had eaten, saying, 'This cup is the new covenant in my blood, which will be shed for you'" (Luke 22:19–20).

+ *Praying for others during His suffering on the Cross:* "Then Jesus said, 'Father, forgive them, they know not what they do'" (Luke 23:34).

+ *With His last breath on earth:* "Father, into your hands I commend my spirit" (Luke 23:46).

+ *Most importantly, Jesus taught us how to pray to God His Father:* "This is how you are to pray: Our Father in heaven, hallowed be your name, your kingdom come, your will be done, on earth as in heaven. Give us today our daily bread; and forgive us our debts, as we forgive our debtors; and do not subject us to the final test, but deliver us from the evil one" (Matt. 6:9–13).

Many holy ones have told us the importance of persistent prayer. St. Vincent de Paul wrote, "Give me a man of prayer, and he will be capable of everything." St. Maximilian Kolbe wrote, "Prayer is still a little known means; however, it is the most effective way to reestablish peace in our souls because it allows us to get even closer to God's love."[37] St. James stated, "The fervent prayer of a righteous person is very powerful." (James 5:16).

The fundamentals of a strong prayer life are simple:

+ *Pray privately in His presence.* Find a quiet place to pray, where you are alone with God. Display an image of Jesus with His Sacred Heart or a crucifix. Recognize that you are in His presence. Don't be like the hypocrites who love to pray out loud and be noticed by others. God, Who sees you in secret, will listen to you (Matt. 6:5–6).

+ *Exercise patience.* In our world today, we have little patience for delay. We have the expectation that our requests will be answered instantly. God doesn't work this way. He works in *His* time. He is always listening to us. We must be patient. The psalmist wrote, "Be still before the LORD; wait for him" (Ps. 37:7).

+ *Practice endless perseverance.* St. Monica was married and the mother of three children. Her husband was a pagan named Patricius. She prayed for thirty years for his conversion. He converted to the Faith a year before his death. Also, she prayed for seventeen years for her son Augustine before he was converted. This young man, now known as St. Augustine, became a Doctor of the Church for his many writings. St. Monica is revered for her endless prayers for her husband and family.[38] Never

---

[37] "These Saints Teach Us the Importance of Prayer," Aleteia, https://aleteia.org/slideshow/slideshow-these-saints-teach-us-the-importance-of-prayer/.

[38] "Saint Monica," Marypages, https://www.marypages.com/saint-monica-en.html.

lose heart in your prayers. St. Paul said, "Pray without ceasing" (1 Thess. 5:17).

+ *Offer thanks to Jesus for considering your prayers.* St. Paul emphasizes the importance of being thankful to Our Lord for listening to our prayers. He wrote, "Have no anxiety at all, but in everything, by prayer and petition, with thanksgiving, make your requests known to God. Then the peace of God that surpasses all understanding will guard your hearts and minds in Christ Jesus" (Phil. 4:6–7).

Mother Angelica had a wonderful approach to prayer. She said,

I have a special relationship with Jesus. He's my Savior, my Love, and I talk to Him, as a friend would speak to a friend. I speak to the Spirit as an intimate confidant, a friend you can talk to about anything. You have to remember, the Church teaches that when you speak to one member of the Trinity, you speak to the entire Trinity. There is no jealousy among Them. So pick the Father, Son, or Holy Spirit, and start talking.[39]

Bishop Robert Baker wrote a fabulous book addressing prayer at our most challenging times in life. When these challenges arise, our response can often be, "Why, Lord?" The bishop gives us the spiritual guidance for these times:

When confronted with the prayer "Why Lord?" we can choose any number of solutions, from seeking counsel from a wise priest to talking with a seasoned counselor or someone who has suffered as we have. But don't forget the One who said, "I am the way." Meditations on His Way

---

[39] Arroyo, *Mother Angelica's Little Book of Life Lessons*, 86.

of the Cross can move us spiritually to link our quandary, our question, our heaviness of hearts, and our suffering with that of Jesus—and if we are patient, He will most likely, in turn, put in our heart trust and resignation to God's holy will by making us realize how great is God's love for us.[40]

Over the centuries, many different ways to pray have developed. Varying our forms of prayer will keep us always stimulated to maintain a persistent prayer life. Some of the kinds of prayer to consider are:

+ *Daily examen of conscience*: St. Ignatius Loyola gave us this process to evaluate our performance in serving Our Lord each day and to see where He was active in our lives. The first step is to acknowledge that you are in the presence of God. Then think about the ways that you were blessed by Him. Next, examine your day from start to finish, thinking about the times when God was present for you in both small and large things. Then express sorrow to Him for any sins you have committed and seek forgiveness. Finally, seek grace from God for the next day.[41]

+ *Pray for others*: Pray for your family, friends, or acquaintances who are suffering physically, psychologically, spiritually, or emotionally. Ask Our Lord to bless these souls with a speedy recovery from their suffering so they can return to serve Him in the special mission

---

[40] Bishop Robert J. Baker, *Prayers of Desperation: A Questioner's Prayer for Answers in Our Darkest Moments* (Irondale, AL: EWTN Publishing, 2023), chap. 1.

[41] "The Ignatian Examen."

He has for them living an abundant life. Also, pray for the deceased that have made a difference in your life, that they are in Heaven and, if not yet, pray that Jesus blesses them with eternal life in accordance with His will. St. Thomas Aquinas emphasized the importance of praying for the souls in Purgatory. He said, "Of all prayers... the most acceptable to God are prayers for the dead, because they imply all the works of charity, both corporal and spiritual."[42]

+ *Pray traditional rote prayers*: The simplest prayers are the Our Father, the Hail Mary, and the Glory Be. Pray the Rosary as often as you can, meditating on the Joyful, Sorrowful, Glorious, or Luminous Mysteries. There are hundreds of other rote prayers which can be found on a free app known as Laudate.

+ *Prayerful reading of Scripture*: Our Lord speaks to those who study His teachings. Try reading one of the Gospels, taking one chapter a day. Consider analyzing the chapters, utilizing the Benedictine process of review known as *Lectio Divina*. The steps are simple: read a passage of Scripture, meditate on the meaning, pray to Our Lord in your own words, and contemplate ways we can be transformed by God's grace to do His will. Pope Benedict XVI recommended this method of review in *Verbum Domini*, 87.

+ *Contemplative prayer*: Take the time to be alone with Our Lord, sharing your thoughts about anything and

---

[42] Quoted in "Why Pray for the Souls in Purgatory?," Littlest Souls, November 6, 2014, https://littlestsouls.wordpress.com/2014/11/06/why-pray-for-the-souls-in-purgatory/.

everything as between friends. Don't hesitate to bare your soul to Him, for He is our God and maker (Psalm 95:6–7). We are hearing the Word of God as His unconditional servant. We say *yes* to Him (CCC 2709, 2716).

+ *Form a prayer group*: In the last several years, small prayer groups have been formed to pray the Rosary, study the Bible, and read Christian books. During these meetings, holy conversation occurs, sharing ideas and thoughts that help the participants grow in their faith and spirituality. Jesus tells us that, "where two or three are gathered together in my name, there am I in the midst of them" (Matt. 18:20).

+ *Adoration time*: In recent times, many parishes around the world have built Adoration chapels, which allow individuals to pray in silence before the Blessed Sacrament, either exposed or in the tabernacle. During Adoration, we acknowledge that God is the Creator and Savior, the Lord and Master of everything that exists and has infinite and merciful love. We recognize that we would not exist but for God. He sets us free from "the slavery of sin and the idolatry of the world." We can pray to Him about anything (CCC 2096, 2097).

+ *Pray the Liturgy of the Hours*: This form of prayer is intended to be the prayer of the whole people of God. It is devised so that the participant can pray throughout the day and night in the praise of God. It consists of Psalms, Psalm prayers, Scripture readings, a responsory, different canticles, intercessions, the Our Father prayer, and a closing prayer (CCC 1174, 1175).

+ *Keep a personal journal of your reflections*: As we travel along our spiritual journey in life, we encounter all kinds of situations, challenges, and blessings from Our Lord. Recording these events in a journal and later reflecting on them helps us in our spiritual growth as we see the will of Jesus at work in our lives.

Excuses, excuses, excuses! Many offer all kinds of excuses for failing to pray or to justify a limited prayer life. Some say their prayer life is dry and boring, that they get distracted easily, they don't get anything out of it, there is not enough time in the day, or God didn't give them what they asked for and they quit. Shame on us for any excuse! The powerful persistent prayer life that Jesus demonstrated on earth and that of the saints clearly proves that a strong prayer life ensures a *wonderful* life.

Parents have a golden opportunity to instill in their children the importance of a strong prayer life. Praying with them before meals and at bedtime is critical to their spiritual development. Our son Blake and his wife, Ashley, pray with their children, Evan and Clare, at bedtime each night, reciting rote prayers and asking them whom they want to pray for. When our son Grant was a little boy, his nightly prayer list often included his pet turtles, Spike, Speedy, and Zephyr.

All of us fall on a spectrum as to our prayer lives with Jesus. There are those who only have a surface relationship with Our Lord, and others have a mature one. Characteristics of a surface relationship are praying occasionally (usually only when we have a need), little or no thanksgiving for His blessings to us, using simple prayers with no dialogue with Our Lord, and bouncing around between joy and unhappiness. There is nothing wrong with a surface relationship with Jesus, but we are missing out on a huge opportunity in life.

By contrast, the characteristics of a mature relationship with Jesus are praying throughout the day and night as Jesus tells us in the Gospels, utilizing the multiple different forms of prayer, learning to listen to the voice of Jesus, and being aware of His presence operating our souls. If we practice a mature prayer relationship with Jesus, our daily lives will be filled with many fruits such as continuous joy, peace, and happiness. He will give us daily direction in all decision-making and the courage to handle adversity. We will have unlimited grace and the self-discipline to avoid temptation. Finally, we will live worry and stress free and experience God's saving power.

Today is the day to commit to a more mature relationship with Jesus by a persistent prayer life. St. Peter tells us about this commitment: "Therefore, brothers, be all the more eager to make your call and election firm, for, in doing so, you will never stumble. For, in this way, entry into the eternal kingdom of our Lord and savior Jesus Christ will be richly provided for you" (2 Pet. 1:10–11).

In simple terms, a life of prayer is the habit of being in the presence of God and in communion with Him (CCC 2565). Once we get into this habit, it means building and maintaining a mature relationship with Jesus and living an awesome life. We will never fall back into a limited prayer life because it is too painful to be without Our Lord at the helm of our lives. The most important part of the day will become our prayer time with Jesus.

Spiritual Treasures for Reflection

Rising very early before dawn, he left and went off to a deserted place, where he prayed. (Mark 1:35; see also Matt. 14:23)

So you could not keep watch with me for one hour? Watch and pray that you may not undergo the test. The spirit is willing, but the flesh is weak. (Matt. 26:40–41)

Give me a man of prayer, and he will be capable of everything. (St. Vincent de Paul)

Teaching #12

Modeling Our Families after the Values of the Holy Family

Grace from God: The return of holiness to our families

A young man in his mid-twenties lost his way in life. He came from a broken family: his parents divorced when he was five years old, his father abandoned the family, and he and his three older siblings were raised by their single mother. He was exposed to alcohol and drugs in his early teens and developed a substance-abuse problem. Despite many efforts, he was unable to resolve this problem.

His mother learned about the Cenacolo Community, which was started by Mother Elvira Petrozzi in 1983. It is a program that helps young men overcome substance abuse. The culture of this organization is a Christian family environment that relies upon the values of prayer, work, friendship, sacrifice, and love. There are seventy-two Cenacolo houses in twenty countries around the world.

The young man thrived in the Cenacolo Community. After spending a year there, he completed his education, married, and now has a wonderful job. The culture of the Cenacolo Community fulfilled the values that were missing in his family. These values are the keys to a successful family. This community has thousands of similar success stories.

The Holy Family—Jesus, His Blessed Mother Mary, and St. Joseph—is the role model for all families. This family had a great culture filled with Christian values where all of the family members could thrive and fulfill God's mission assignment for each of them. These values are the difference between a family being holy or dysfunctional. The Holy Family is so important that our Church celebrates a feast day for it every year between Christmas and New Year's Day. A common practice is to write the letters "JMJ"—Jesus, Mary, Joseph—at the top of correspondence and memos, in memory of the Holy Family.

Our Blessed Mother Mary and St. Joseph practiced the Christian values of prayer, self-discipline, great work ethic, sacrifice, and love. They taught Jesus to live a strong spiritual life, which included the study of Old Testament Scriptures and always doing the will of God the Father. St. Joseph taught Jesus the skills of a carpenter and how to work with others. Our Lady emphasized the importance of obedience to parents and that the favor of God was upon Him. This family was pure and free from sin. Love was at the center of their lives.

The fundamental elements of a holy family are described by Jesus in the Gospels and in many books of the Old Testament, the New Testament, and the *Catechism of the Catholic Church*. The first element is to practice our Faith. St. Paul said, "Believe in the Lord Jesus and you and your household will be saved" (Acts 16:31). The prophet Joshua wrote, "As for me and my household, we will serve the LORD" (Joshua 24:15). To practice our Faith requires the family to pray together every day, especially at meals. Reading Christian books with your children before they fall asleep will educate them in their Faith. Ask them to pray for others who need Our Lord's help to teach them compassion. As they become teenagers, set aside a day each week to pray the Rosary or read the Bible together. Prayer time with them as youngsters will help prayer become a habit for a lifetime.

Going to Mass on Sundays emphasizes the importance of partaking of the Eucharist for spiritual strength and growth for the family. They will hear Scripture references and reflections upon them. Participating at Mass as altar servers, lectors, and Eucharistic ministers will help family members build a strong family bond tied to their Faith.

The second element is that love must be at the core of family life. St. Paul describes what love truly is for our families. He says, "Love is patient, love is kind. It is not jealous, love is not pompous, it is not inflated, it is not rude, it does not seek its own interests, it is not quick-tempered, it does not brood over injury, it does not rejoice over wrongdoing.... It bears all things, believes all things, hopes all things, endures all things. Love never fails" (1 Cor. 13:4-8).

Another fundamental requirement is to fully comprehend the responsibilities of each family member toward one another. It all begins with the relationship of husband and wife. When a man leaves his family and clings to his wife, the two of them become one body (Gen. 2:24). "What God has joined together, no human being must separate" (Mark 10:9). Husbands and wives must commit to the practice of the Faith and then pursue it together. Husbands have an obligation to love their wives even as Christ loves the Church (Eph. 5:25). Furthermore, husbands are to avoid any bitterness toward their wives (Col. 3:19). Wives are to respect their husbands (Eph. 5:33).

Parents have the duty to train their children in the way they should conduct themselves; even when they get older, they will not turn from it (Prov. 22:6). This duty to help their children is a fundamental requirement (CCC 2221). Parents must recognize their obligation to educate their children in practicing the Faith and to provide for their physical and spiritual needs (CCC 2226, 2228). They are to practice the virtues (CCC 2223). Tenderness, fidelity, respect, and selflessness must be exercised as the norm (CCC 2222–2223). They are not to provoke their children to anger or discourage them (Eph. 6:4; Col. 3:21).

Parents are to serve as role models for their children, who often imitate them. Children should be encouraged by their parents to participate in different activities in order to develop their social skills and knowledge of the world. They are to monitor the individuals their children befriend in order to protect them against negative influences. Parents have the obligation to be true shepherds of their children.

Children have duties toward their parents. One of the Ten Commandments is to honor your father and mother (Exod. 20:12). Children have the duty to honor the commands of their father and to follow the teaching of their mothers (Prov. 6:20). They have a duty to be obedient to their parents (Prov. 1:8 and 6:20). Children have the duty to walk in the Truth (3 John 1:4). Also, children have the responsibility to take care of their parents as they grow old, even if their minds fail (Sirach 3:13–16).

Siblings can get sideways with one another. But they have an obligation to bear with each other and show forgiveness as needed, just as Our Lord does for us (Col. 3:13). Brothers and sisters must love one another, just as God loves us (1 John 4:21).

Once we learn and pursue the first three fundamental elements of a holy family—practicing our Faith, putting love at the core of our family life, and observing the responsibilities of each family member—the last element is to be obedient to the will of God at all times. The Holy Family showed us the way. They were totally obedient to God's will. Our Blessed Mother Mary said *yes* to be the Mother of Jesus. She responded to the request from the angel Gabriel with these words: "Behold, I am the handmaid of the Lord. May it be done to me according to your word" (Luke 1:38). St. Joseph agreed to be the husband of Mary and earthly father of Jesus (Matt. 1:18–24). Jesus voluntarily left the joys of Heaven to come to earth as our Messiah and to show us the way to eternal salvation (Matt. 1:16; John 3:16).

Families who practice these fundamental elements of a holy family create a strong culture in which joy and happiness flourish. Husbands and wives will have a great life together. Children will have a strong spiritual life, doing the will of Jesus as a way of life. Siblings will create lasting relationships that will benefit them for the rest of their lives.

Sadly, many families in our culture today have strayed from the fundamentals of a holy family and are dysfunctional. Destroying the family unit by the plagues of divorce, relativism, and secularization are common now. The desire for material wealth often consumes parents, causing them to ignore the responsibility of properly raising their children. Many families are run by a single parent, as the other parent has abandoned their obligations. Children are often the subject of abuse or neglect. The emphasis has become the well-being of the individual and not the family unit. Selfishness has replaced selflessness.

If you are a member of a dysfunctional family, it is never too late to work diligently to bring everyone in line with the fundamentals of a holy family. St. Paul gives us direction in this situation:

> Put on then, as God's chosen ones, holy and beloved, heartfelt compassion, kindness, humility, gentleness, and

patience, bearing with one another and forgiving one another, if one has a grievance against another; as the Lord has forgiven you, so must you also do.... Let the peace of Christ control your hearts, the peace into which you were also called in one body.... And whatever you do, in word or in deed, do everything in the name of the Lord Jesus, giving thanks to God the Father through him. (Col. 3:12–17)

Pope St. John Paul II emphasized the importance of the family many times during his papacy. He declared 1994 as the International Year of the Family. In his *Letter to Families*, he wrote, "The family is indeed—more than any other social reality—the place where an individual can exist 'for himself' through the sincere gift of self. This is why it remains a social institution that neither can nor should be replaced: it is the 'sanctuary of life.'" A year later in his encyclical *Evangelium Vitae*, he wrote, "Within the 'people of life and the people for life,' the family has a decisive responsibility.... Here it is a matter of God's own love, of which parents are co-workers and as it were interpreters when they transmit life and raise it according to His Fatherly plan."

All of us remember the crazy times created by the COVID-19 pandemic. Amazingly, one positive impact of this experience was that many families grew closer together. According to the U.S. Census Bureau's 2020 Survey of Income and Program Participation (SIPP), many families spent more time together amidst the lockdowns that were in place. Parents shared dinners and read to their children more frequently than before.[43] Hopefully, now that

---

[43] Yerís Mayol-García, "Pandemic Brought Parents and Children Closer," *Lake County News*, January 6, 2022, https://www.lakeconews

we are in the post-pandemic era, this family growth will continue in the future.

Over the years of serving as a permanent deacon in the Archdiocese of New Orleans in Good Shepherd Parish, I have been blessed with the opportunity to serve as officiant for numerous weddings and Baptisms. Inspired by the Holy Spirit, I explain to husbands and wives that it is their primary duty to do all that they can to get one another to Heaven. Similarly, parents are advised that it is their responsibility to do everything possible to help their children reach Heaven. As we have learned from the teachings of Jesus, the books of the Old and New Testaments, the *Catechism of the Catholic Church*, and the writings of the saints, the only way to achieve this ultimate goal in life is for the culture of our families to be filled with love and happiness, practicing our Faith, fulfilling the role of each family member, listening, and being obedient to the will of God. We must practice the values of the Holy Family.

.com/news/71393-pandemic-brought-parents-and-children-closer-more-family-dinners-more-reading-to-young-children.

Spiritual Treasures for Reflection

Believe in the Lord Jesus and you and your household will be saved. (Acts 16:31)

Train the young in the way they should go; even when old, they will not swerve from it. (Prov. 22:6)

The family is indeed—more than any other social reality—the place where an individual can exist 'for himself' through the sincere gift of self. This is why it remains a social institution that neither can nor should be replaced: it is the "sanctuary of life." (Pope St. John Paul II)

Teaching #13

Managing the Two Elephants in the Room: Suffering and Death

Grace from God: Courage and peace from the Holy Spirit
for the most challenging times in life

Suffering: A Necessary Part of Life

St. Maximilian Kolbe was born in Poland in 1894. At age twelve, he had a vision of our Blessed Mother, Mary, who asked him if he wanted to wear either a white crown or a red one. The white one represented a life of purity, and the red one meant that he would become a martyr. The saint told the Virgin Mary that he was willing to wear both of them. He later joined the order of conventional Franciscans. In his priestly ministry, he promoted devotion to Our Lady, operated a publishing business, and started several monasteries.

Germany invaded Poland in 1939. He opened a temporary hospital to help people suffering, provided shelter for refugees, and issued many anti-German publications. He was arrested by the German Gestapo and brought to Pawiak prison and later transferred to Auschwitz. While there, many men were chosen to go through death by starvation. One of the men selected was a man with a family. The saint fulfilled the red crown of suffering and martyrdom he promised to our Blessed Mother Mary and voluntarily took the place of the family man. During the starvation time, he said prayers to the Virgin Mary with the other prisoners. After two weeks, he was given a lethal injection. St. Maximilian Kolbe was canonized by Pope John Paul II in 1982 and declared a martyr. (Catholic Online, "Saints & Angels: St. Maximilian Kolbe").

This martyr of the Church utilized the tools from Jesus to manage his suffering and death by execution, as he was obedient to the will of God, selfless as he gave up his life, complaint free, engaged in prayer, and forgiving of his executioners.

There are many certainties in life. Some of them are suffering and death. Our culture tends to focus our attention on the good times in this earthly life, while ignoring these certainties. It is important to directly address suffering and death to learn how to manage them when our time comes. Every soul has a choice to make. Are we going to manage our end time following the ways of Jesus, His Blessed Mother Mary, and martyrs like St. Maximilian Kolbe? Or are we going to fight it, making those around us miserable? Since we believe that those who live the teachings of Jesus reach Heaven, one must manage the suffering as Jesus taught us.

The tools Jesus gave us for suffering are:

+ *Be obedient.* During His public ministry, Jesus had many conversations with His apostles about His teachings. In one of them, He described His coming suffering, saying, "The Son of Man must suffer greatly and be rejected by the elders, the chief priests, and the scribes, and be killed and on the third day be raised" (Luke 9:22). Our Lord was obedient to the will of His Father and willingly accepted His Passion and Crucifixion. Jesus further gave us instruction to be obedient to the will of His Father as to the suffering that all of us will experience. He said, "If anyone wishes to come after me, he must deny himself and take up his cross daily and follow me" (Luke 9:23).

+ *Exercise selflessness.* Our Lord taught us to be selfless when our time of suffering comes, thinking of others and not ourselves. While carrying His Cross on the way to His Crucifixion, Jesus could have complained to those around Him about His awful suffering. Instead, He comforted the crowds who followed Him, saying, "Daughters of Jerusalem, do not weep for me" (Luke 23:28). As Jesus was near death, He consoled a criminal who was hanging next to Him, saying, "Amen, I say to you, today you will be with me in Paradise" (Luke 23:43). Being selfless gives us the grace we need to handle any kind of suffering.

+ *Never complain.* One of the most amazing things about the suffering of Jesus at the end of His life was that He never complained. His Passion and Crucifixion are documented in each of the four Gospels. His strength, perseverance, and endurance were beyond words. There is no other role model who can compare to Our Lord.

+ *Develop a strong prayer life.* Prayer was a hallmark of the life of Jesus on earth. His daily encounters with God through prayer served Him perfectly when His most critical time of need arose in the agony in the Garden of Gethsemane. Our Lord was praying to His Father about His upcoming Passion and Crucifixion. During this time, His sweat was like droplets of blood falling on the ground (Luke 22:44). Through His dialogue with His Father, He freely accepted His coming torture and execution. God gave Him the divine grace to manage this incredible time of suffering. There is zero doubt about the importance of a strong daily prayer life with Jesus to help us in our earthly challenges and at our most critical time, the hour of our suffering and death. Please don't wait until that hour comes to develop a strong prayer life!

+ *Forgiveness of others.* Sometimes our suffering is caused by others. A natural response would be to retaliate and want to harm those who have hurt us. However, Jesus gives us clear direction on how to manage suffering caused by others. When He was hanging on the Cross, He asked God to forgive those who tortured Him, saying, "Father, forgive them, they know not what they do" (Luke 23:34). Jesus further told us that forgiveness of others is endless, saying we are to forgive others as much as seventy times seven (see Matt. 18:21–22).

+ *Allow the Holy Spirit to work in you.* This third member of the Holy Trinity provides us with many great gifts and fruits that are readily available to us. One of the gifts is the courage to handle any type of challenge that comes our way, including suffering. He further provides us with the fruits of peace, patience, and self-control to manage our pain and suffering. Don't hesitate to put the power of the Holy Spirit at work in you when the challenging times come.

All of us must recognize and accept that suffering and challenges are a part of life. They come to us in many different forms. There is physical suffering, such as injury, disease, physical ailments, dementia, substance abuse, and the effects of aging. We can experience it in the workplace in the form of a job loss, reduction in wages, bias, an oppressive boss, or a loss of business. There is mental health suffering, such as anxiety, depression, and other types. Spiritual issues can arise which cause suffering, such as sins caused by pride, anger, lust, laziness, jealousy, greed, gluttony, being mean-spirited to others, and loss of our faith. Emotional challenges can arise, such as disagreements with your spouse, family members, or friends, which lead to hatred and a loss of a relationship. Issues arise in caring for others, especially in being a caretaker for a parent or spouse with advanced dementia or a terminal disease. Death of a loved one such as a parent, spouse, child, brother, or sister can arise, which can present many challenges. Being a victim of a catastrophe such as a hurricane, tornado, earthquake, or other event of nature causes seemingly endless suffering. In addition, we can be wrongly criticized by others or bullied because of our beliefs. When these times arise, we need to utilize the tools that Jesus gave us to manage the suffering and challenges.

Many saints have taught us about how to think about suffering. St. Maria Faustina Kowalska was a religious in the congregation of the Sisters of Our Lady of Mercy. She is regarded as one of the outstanding mystics of the Church. She suffered a physically agonizing death from tuberculosis and internal hemorrhaging at the age of thirty-three. St. Maria kept a diary of her communications with Jesus. She wrote, "Suffering is the greatest treasure on earth; it purifies the soul. In suffering, we learn who is our true friend. True love is measured by the thermometer of suffering" (*Diary* 342).

This saint offered us prayer to Jesus to help us when suffering arises. She wrote, "Jesus, I thank You for the little daily crosses, for opposition to my endeavors, for the hardships of communal life, for the misrepresentation of my intentions, for humiliations at the hands of others, for the harsh way in which we are treated, for false suspicions, for poor health and loss of strength, for self-denial, for dying to myself, for lack of recognition in everything, for the upsetting of all my plans.... I thank You, Jesus, You who first drank the cup of bitterness before You gave it to me, in a much milder form. (*Diary* 342–343)

St. Rita of Cascia was born in Italy in 1381. Although she desired to enter the religious life, her parents forced her into an arranged marriage to a cruel man. During their twenty years of married life, she prayed for his conversion. He was murdered shortly after this conversion. Thereafter, her two sons became ill and died. Despite all this suffering, she never gave up on her faith. Subsequently, she entered the Augustinian convent. While there, she suffered illness and a continuous open wound on her forehead. She accepted this suffering, relying upon grace from God and considering it similar to Jesus when He was crowned with thorns during His passion.[44]

Mother Angelica suffered greatly during her lifetime. She experienced many ailments, including diabetes, an enlarged heart, a twisted spine, lame legs, and asthma. She experienced some type of suffering every day, and she offers us very comforting ways to think about it. She said, "

I don't remember a day, even before I knew Jesus, when I didn't have a problem, when I didn't have pain. And I realized it was a privilege.... Everybody suffers in the world. Whether I am suffering in a physical, mental, or spiritual manner, I resemble Jesus at those moments, and the Father looks at us in our pain and He sees His Son in the most beautiful way. That's what makes you holy. Don't rebel.[45]

[44] "The 4 Patron Saints of Impossible Causes," Good Catholic, https://www.goodcatholic.com/patron-saints-of-impossible-causes/.
[45] Arroyo, *Mother Angelica's Little Book of Life Lessons*, 111, 219.

Rest assured that Our Lord will provide you with all of the grace that you need when challenges come your way. Grace is defined as "favor, the free and undeserved help that God gives us to respond to his call to become children of God" (CCC 1996). St. Paul tells us about this grace: "No trial has come to you but what is human. God is faithful and will not let you be tried beyond your strength; but with the trial he will also provide a way out, so that you may be able to bear it" (1 Cor. 10:13).

Our Lord may provide you with an angel to help you in your greatest suffering. When Jesus was agonizing in the Garden of Gethsemane over His coming Crucifixion, an angel from Heaven appeared to Him to give Him strength (Luke 22:41-43).

My mother, Mary Eason, was diagnosed with terminal cancer in 1999. There were no treatments available to save her. During her six months of suffering, she had major weight loss from 120 to about 80 pounds. She was very calm and freely accepted this suffering. One night when I was visiting with her, I asked how she was able to manage it. She said she received many graces from Our Lord, including an appearance from her guardian angel. She told me that the name of her angel was the same as her first name—however, it was spelled slightly different: Meri. Her guardian angel comforted her all during her suffering. Mom desperately wanted to make it to Christmas morning that year to give gifts to her grandchildren. She made it to Christmas Day and died that night.

St. Padre Pio entered the Capuchin Friary of Morcone (Benevento), Italy, at the age of fifteen. In 1910, at the age of twenty-three, he was given the wounds of Christ—the stigmata. These wounds were invisible for several years. In 1918, he had a vision of Jesus and was given the visible stigmata in his hands, feet, and side. Thereafter, many people began to visit him at the friary for Confession. Numerous folks were cured through the intercession of this saint. He is well known for his relationship with his guardian angel throughout his lifetime.

St. Padre Pio experienced suffering from the stigmata for nearly sixty years. This special saint wrote a prayer known as Stay with Me Lord, which states in part:

> Stay with me, Lord, for it is necessary to have You present so that I do not forget You. You know how easily I abandon You. Stay with me, Lord, because I am weak and I need Your strength, that I may not fall so often. Stay with me, Lord, for You are my life, and without You, I am without fervor. Stay with me, Lord, for You are my light, and without You, I am in darkness. Stay with me, Lord, to show me Your will. Stay with me, Lord, so that I can hear Your voice and follow You.... With a firm love, I will love You with all my heart while on earth and continue to love You perfectly during all eternity. Amen![46]

Suffering is a certainty in life. We experience it along the way in our journey. It comes in many different forms. Sometimes we can see it coming our way, other times it comes as a surprise. When it comes, we have to use the tools Jesus gave us during His time on earth. Attitude about suffering is everything. It is most important that we thank Jesus, Who first drank the cup of suffering before He gave it to us in a much milder form (*Diary* 343).

Death: Passing to Eternal Life in Heaven

There are all kinds of warnings in our world. Traffic signs help drivers navigate highways safely. A stop sign requires a motorist to

---

[46] "Stay with Me, Lord," Padre Pio Devotions, https://padrepiodevotions.org/stay-with-me-lord/.

stop at an intersection to check for oncoming vehicles. A flashing yellow light at a highway crossing informs drivers to slow down and proceed with caution. There are signs on the edge of a swimming pool, alerting swimmers not to dive because of shallow water. Many consumer products have warnings on them to prevent injury and property damage. The purpose of all these warnings is to get our attention and to change our behavior in some way.

In Mark's Gospel, Jesus gives us a warning about the end times. He says, "But of that day or hour, no one knows, neither the angels in heaven, nor the Son, but only the Father" (Mark 13:32). St. Paul further warns us about the end of our lives in death. He wrote, "For you yourselves know very well that the day of the Lord will come like a thief at night.... Therefore, let us not sleep as the rest do, but let us stay alert and sober" (1 Thess. 5:2, 6). Based on these warnings, we must keep our souls vigilant by living in a state of grace, doing the will of Jesus, always being ready for the time when Jesus calls us from this life. Remember what the priest tells us when we receive ashes on Ash Wednesday: "Remember, man, you are dust and to dust you will return."[47]

Death can come at any age. It can happen in childbirth, as a child or teenager, during the prime of life, or in old age. There are many causes. It can be natural, from disease such as cancer, stroke, or a failing heart. Death can occur by accident, from a vehicle collision or plane crash. It can occur by tragedy, from a tornado or hurricane. Sometimes it occurs instantly with no warning or gradually over a period of time. In all instances, we must have our souls prepared to pass to eternal life in Heaven with God the Father, Our Lord Jesus, and the Holy Spirit.

[47] Pope St. John Paul II, "Remember You Are Dust," homily for Ash Wednesday 1996.

Spiritual Lightning

To illustrate the importance of being prepared for death, Our Lord tells us the parable of the ten virgins who went out to meet the bridegroom. Five of them were wise. They were prepared, as they had their lamps filled with oil. The other five were foolish, as they had no oil in their lamps. At midnight, the bridegroom arrived. The wise virgins went out to greet the bridegroom with their lamps. The foolish ones missed this opportunity because they had to leave to buy oil from nearby merchants. The bridegroom invited the wise virgins into the wedding feast and then locked the doors. Afterward, the other virgins came and said, "Lord, Lord, open the door for us!" He replied, "Amen, I say to you, I do not know you." From this parable, Our Lord tells us to be prepared. "Stay awake, for you know neither the day nor the hour" (Matt. 25:11-13).

The Good News is that we have the opportunity to be prepared for the end of our earthly lives. We can pay attention to the warnings from Jesus and modify our way of life as needed. We can leave behind the hardness of our hearts and weakness of our souls to a new life where we follow His values, allowing us to produce much fruit. Jesus tells us that we can be like the growth of the fig tree. As the branches transition from hard to tender before summer, they begin to produce much fruit (Mark 13:28).

We all want to make the cut to reach heaven with Our Lord forever. Accomplishing this goal is a simple concept. We have to replace vices of anger, gluttony, lust, pride, laziness, envy, and greed with the virtues of faith, hope, charity, courage, prudence, justice, and temperance. We must allow the Holy Spirit to direct all of our actions, doing the will of Jesus at all times.

In our lives, we spend much of our time working on our earthly résumés. A résumé lists our education, work history, and significant accomplishments. However, to successfully pass from this life to Heaven, we want the best possible spiritual résumé. Our spiritual résumés need to contain strong evidence of our efforts doing the will of Our Lord and spreading the Good News to others. It is important that we have a good history of being selfless helping others and doing the corporal works of mercy—such as feeding the hungry, giving drink to the thirsty, clothing the naked, sheltering the homeless, visiting the sick and imprisoned, burying the dead, and giving alms to the poor (CCC 2447). Have we participated in church ministry and community activities? It is also important to partake of the Sacraments of the Eucharist and Confession regularly. We want to "compete well for the faith," to "lay hold of eternal life" to which we are all called (1 Tim. 6:12). St. Paul tells us that on the day of Christ, we don't want to have run the race or labored in vain (Phil. 2:16).

We all must heed the warning from Jesus seriously because at our judgment we will have to account for how we spent our time on this earth (Heb. 9:27). Jesus will ask us this question: "What did you do with the talents I gave you to make the world a better place?" How will our Lord respond to our answer to this question? Will He say, "Well done, my good and faithful servant.... Come, share your master's joy"? (Matt. 25:23). Or will He respond, "You wicked, lazy servant!... Throw this useless servant into the darkness outside, where there will be wailing and grinding of teeth" (Matt. 25:26, 30)?

Fear of death is a natural human feeling. However, Our Lord teaches us to eliminate fear, replacing it with willing acceptance of the end of our lives and with courage and peace from the Holy Spirit. He demonstrated this for us in the Garden of Gethsemane. His initial reluctance to experience His Passion and Crucifixion was replaced with a desire to do the will of God His Father. He said, "Father, if you are willing, take this cup away from me; still, not my will but yours be done" (Luke 22:42). Our Lord embraced His suffering courageously in peace, relying upon the gifts and fruits from the Holy Spirit. Jesus was an example for us so we can follow in His footsteps (1 Pet. 2:21).

My mother-in-law, Mary Ann Doyle, passed away at the age of ninety. Her health declined in the last several years of her life. She suffered from heart failure, thyroid issues, major orthopedic pain, and cancer. She was upbeat despite her suffering and seldom complained. She lived in an assisted living facility for several years and was a role model for the patients and staff there. She had great faith and prayed the Rosary every day. She told me many times that she wasn't afraid to die. She demonstrated wonderful courage and peace at the end of her life.

When death arrives, we are not alone. Our Lord is with us. "I command you; be strong and steadfast! Do not fear nor be dismayed, for the LORD, your God, is with you wherever you go" (Josh. 1:9). The psalmist further acknowledges the presence of Our Lord at the end of life. He writes, "Even though I walk through the valley of the shadow of death, I will fear no evil, for you are with me; your rod and your staff comfort me." (Ps. 23:4).

St. Margaret Mary Alacoque provides us with an insurance policy that ensures that Our Lord will be with us in the final moments. She lived in France in the 1600s and had private revelations from Jesus. In one of them, Our Lord told her of certain promises that He gives to all souls who receive the Eucharist on the first Friday of nine consecutive months. One of the promises for all those who fulfill this request is that they will not die in His displeasure or without receiving the sacraments. Further, His divine heart will be our safe refuge in the last moment.[48]

---

[48] Fr. Edward McNamara, "First Friday Devotion and First Friday," EWTN, March 17, 2015, https://www.ewtn.com/catholicism/library/first-friday-devotion-and-first-friday-4760.

Many people have the mistaken understanding that, once we die, it is the end of our existence—that there is no afterlife. Jesus, the prophet Isaiah, and St. Paul all assure us that upon death, we will transition to the next life. We all have the opportunity to gain Heaven.

Here is the proof:

+ Jesus said, "In my Father's house there are many dwelling places. If there were not, would I have told you that I am going to prepare a place for you? And if I go and prepare a place for you, I will come back again and take you to myself, so that where I am you also may be" (John 14:2-3).

+ Our Lord further said, "Amen, amen, I say to you, whoever keeps my word will never see death" (John 8:51).

+ The prophet Isaiah wrote, "He will destroy death forever. The Lord GOD will wipe away the tears from all faces" (Isa. 25:8).

+ St. Paul wrote, "For since death came through a human being, the resurrection of the dead came also through a human being. For just as in Adam all die, so too in Christ shall all be brought to life" (1 Cor. 15:21-22).

Perhaps the least known sacrament is the Anointing of the Sick. It is available to all of us when there is a danger of death from sickness or old age. It is utilized when someone is facing a major surgery as well (CCC 1514, 1515). The sacrament was instituted by Our Lord as a proper sacrament of the New Testament. It was recommended to the faithful and promulgated by James the apostle (CCC 1511).

The Sacrament of the Anointing of the Sick consists of anointing on the forehead and hands with duly blessed oil. The priest says, "Through this holy anointing may the Lord in his love and mercy help you with the grace of the Holy Spirit. May the Lord who frees you from sin save you and raise you up" (CCC 1513). Special grace comes from the sacrament, which has the effects of uniting the sick person to the Passion of Christ, strengthening, giving the peace and courage to endure sufferings, granting forgiveness of sins if the person was unable to obtain it from the Sacrament of Penance, restoration of health if it is conducive to the salvation of the soul, and preparation for passing to eternal life (CCC 1532). Anointing of the Sick can be received more than once as necessary (CCC 1515).

Death of others impacts us all in different ways. For some, they experience intense emotion and sadness over the loss of a spouse, family member, or close friend. They may grieve for a long period of time. Others feel sorrow over the loss of the person but recognize that the deceased is in a better place with Our Lord. From the Old Testament book of Lamentations, the Lord brings grief and shows compassion according to the abundance of His mercy (Lam. 3:32). He heals the brokenhearted and binds up their wounds (Ps. 147:3). St. Paul tells us that if we have faith, "Jesus died and rose, so too will God, through Jesus, bring with him those who have fallen asleep" (1 Thess. 4:14).

We need to recognize that it is normal to be consumed with sadness by the passing of another. Notwithstanding, we need to recognize the importance of caring for others, even as we grieve. We need to be a rock for them.

My father, Rudy Eason, was the youngest of four boys. All of them served in World War II. My uncle Dick, a Navy fighter pilot, was shot down during a bombing raid over Japan. Another brother, Frank, suffered catastrophic injuries in a car accident and died many months later. When his only remaining brother, Bill, died, my father was in poor health, suffering as a leg amputee with severe heart disease and diabetes. The family was experiencing deep sadness and emotion over Bill's passing. All during the funeral proceedings, my father showed no emotion. Afterward, I asked him how he was able to be so stoic. He told me that someone had to be a rock for the family.

It is easy in life to focus on the good times, failing to think about the end of our time on this earth. It is most critical that we be prepared, as we don't know the day or the hour when our Lord will call us from this life. Preparation is not complicated, yet it can be a challenge to give up temptation and sinful ways. With proper preparation doing the will of Our Lord, when we meet Jesus face-to-face at the time of our judgment, we will hear these words: "Well done, my good and faithful servant.... Come, share your master's joy" (Matt. 25:23). Heaven will be our reward for living the values of Jesus. We don't want to be unprepared and hear His voice tell us, "You wicked, lazy servant!... Throw this useless servant into the darkness outside, where there will be wailing and grinding of teeth" (Matt. 25:26, 30).

Spiritual Treasures for Reflection

No trial has come to you but what is human. God is faithful and will not let you be tried beyond your strength; but with the trial he will also provide a way out, so that you may be able to bear it. (1 Cor. 10:13)

But of that day or hour, no one knows, neither the angels in heaven, nor the Son, but only the Father. (Mark 13:32)

Even though I walk through the valley of the shadow of death, I will fear no evil, for you are with me; your rod and your staff comfort me. (Ps. 23:4)

Teaching #14

Experience the Miraculous Healing Power of God, the Divine Physician

Grace from God: He can heal us both spiritually and physically.

A teenage girl named Mary was living in the town of Nazareth when the angel Gabriel appeared to her. Mary, who was in a state of grace with God, was betrothed to a man named Joseph. God sent the angel Gabriel to appear to Mary with several messages. First, the angel told her, "Behold, you will conceive in your womb and bear a son, and you shall name him Jesus." Mary questioned the angel, "How can this be, since I have no relations with a man?" Gabriel replied, "The holy Spirit will come upon you, and the power of the Most High will overshadow you. Therefore the child to be born will be called holy, the Son of God" (Luke 1:31, 34-35).

The second message from the angel was about Mary's cousin. He told her, "Behold, Elizabeth, your relative, has also conceived a son in her old age, and this is the sixth month for her who was called barren." The last message from the angel informs the whole world about the healing power of God. Gabriel told Mary, "Nothing will be impossible for God" (Luke 1:36-37).

These two miraculous conceptions, by Mary and by Elizabeth in her old age, attest to the great power of God. The Bible is replete with miracles and healings of all kinds to prove that all things are possible for God.

The prophets spoke of the miraculous power of God. Jeremiah wrote, "Ah, my Lord GOD! You made the heavens and the earth with your great power and your outstretched arm; nothing is too difficult for you" (Jer. 32:17). The prophet Job tells us, "In your place, I would appeal to God, and to God I would state my plea. He does things great and unsearchable, things marvelous and innumerable. He gives rain upon the earth and sends water upon the fields; He sets up the lowly on high, and those who mourn are raised to safety" (Job 5:8–11).

The apostles echoed the writings of the prophets. Matthew wrote about the statement of Jesus as to this great power: "Jesus looked at them and said, 'For human beings this is impossible, but for God all things are possible'" (Matt. 19:26). The apostle Mark stated, "Jesus said to him,... 'Everything is possible to one who has faith'" (Mark 9:23).

Let's explore the scope of these awesome miraculous powers of the Holy Trinity to establish that everything is possible by them. The healing miracles of Jesus account for over 20 percent of the Gospels. Matthew wrote, "He went around all of Galilee, teaching in the synagogues, proclaiming the gospel of the Kingdom, and curing every disease and illness among the people" (Matt. 4:23).

These miracles can be described best as either supernatural, physical, or spiritual.

+ *Supernatural*: God creates the world (Gen. 1); Moses parts the Red Sea (Exod. 14:21); manna from Heaven feeds the Israelites (John 6:31–32); Moses taps the rock from which water flows to his people (Exod. 17:1–7); Jesus converts water into wine at a wedding reception (John 2:1-11); Jesus feeds five thousand people from five loaves of bread and two fish (Luke 9:13-17); and Jesus is transfigured into His divine self in the presence of the apostles Peter, James, and John (Luke 9:28-36). The greatest supernatural miracle is the Resurrection of Jesus from the dead (Mark 16:1-20).

+ *Physical*: Jesus heals a blind man (Mark 10:46-52), a sick boy (John 4:46-54), a crippled woman (Luke 13:10-17), a paralyzed man (Mark 2:1-12), a leper (Mark 1:40-45), a woman with a fever (Mark 1:29-34), and a deaf man who has a speech impediment (Mark 7:31-37). In the greatest of His healings, Our Lord raises Lazarus from the dead (John 11:1-44) and does the same for a young girl (Mark 5:34-45).

+ *Spiritual*: God heals the brokenhearted and binds up their wounds (Ps. 147:3). Jesus heals the Samaritan woman at the well from her past misconduct (John 4:5-30). The greatest spiritual miracle is Our Lord's death on the Cross to cure us from our sins (Mark 15:21-41).

Jesus gave His apostles and disciples the authority to intercede for Him to heal His people. He said to them, "Go rather to the lost sheep of the house of Israel. As you go, make this proclamation: 'The kingdom of heaven is at hand.' Cure the sick, raise the dead, cleanse lepers, drive out demons." (Matt. 10:6-8). He further gave instructions to seventy-two of His disciples, "Whatever town you enter and they welcome you, eat what is set before you, cure the sick in it and say to them, 'The kingdom of God is at hand for you'" (Luke 10:8-9).

The Book of Acts written by St. Luke provides accounts of the apostles healing people based on the intercessory power of Jesus. A crippled man was lying at the gate of the temple. Peter was about to enter the gate when he spoke to the man, saying, "In the name of Jesus Christ the Nazorean, [rise and] walk." The man leapt to his feet, began walking, and entered the temple with Peter and John, praising God (Acts 3:1–10). On another occasion, Peter, through his intersession to Jesus, healed a multitude of men and women of their sickness and cured them from unclean spirits (Acts 5:12–16). Similarly, the apostle Philip, through the power of Our Lord, cured many from unclean spirits and healed others who were paralyzed or lame (Acts 8:4–8). Handkerchiefs and aprons that touched St. Paul and taken to the sick cured their illnesses, and evil spirits left them (Acts 19:11–12).

From the time of Jesus, countless healings and miracles have happened through the intercessory power of our Blessed Mother Mary (see teaching #10) and of the saints. Souls can pray to Our Lady and to the saints for a specific healing. They will intercede with Jesus for the request. Our Lord has the power to grant these requests.

In order to be recognized as a saint, there must be a minimum of two miracles that are attributable to their intercession with Our Lord. There are two miracles that have been accepted by the Vatican that are attributable to the intercessory requests of St. Teresa of Calcutta. One is for a woman in India and the other for a man from Brazil. A Miraculous Medal that had been touched to the body of St. Teresa was placed on the stomach of the woman, and her abdominal tumor vanished. As to the other miracle, an engineer in Brazil fell into a coma due to a brain infection. A relic of St. Teresa was placed on his head, and he awoke from the coma, cured of the disease prior to a surgery.[49]

---

[49] Sarah Kettler, "Mother Teresa: The Miracles That Made Her a Saint," Biography, updated October 14, 2020, https://www.biography.com/religious-figures/mother-teresa-miracles-saint.

Sr. Briege McKenna, O.S.C., was a beneficiary of a physical and spiritual healing and has become a special healer through the power of Our Lord. She was born on Pentecost in 1946 in Ireland. She entered the convent on her fifteenth birthday. In 1964, Sister developed severe pain in her feet caused by rheumatoid arthritis. She spent many months in the hospital. Over the next several years, her suffering grew worse as she could barely walk. Her doctor said there was no hope for her and she would be confined to a wheelchair.

On the morning of December 9, 1970, she was in a prayer meeting with a priest. She prayed, "Jesus, please help me." At that moment, she felt a hand touch her head and a power go through her body. It seemed like a banana being peeled. She was healed from her suffering. Sr. Briege jumped up and screamed, "Jesus, you're right here!" This was truly a miraculous healing, but her greatest healing was her spiritual life. She experienced the release of the great power of the Holy Spirit in her soul.

On the eve of Pentecost in June 1971, Sister went to the chapel in the convent for a holy hour. She was there for about five minutes when she looked at the tabernacle and heard a voice say to her, "You have my gift of healing. Go and use it." That morning, this same message was booming in her head. That day, she visited a hospital and prayed to Jesus for a miracle for a child who was later healed.

Since that day in 1971, by the power of Jesus, numerous souls have been healed physically and spiritually through the intercession of Sr. McKenna. She is merely an instrument of healing. She prays for people by phone from anywhere. The physical healings from her intercession with Our Lord include those with cancer, polio, burns, addictions, marriage difficulties, brain tumors, and other ailments.[50]

---

[50] Briege McKenna, O.S.C., *Miracles Do Happen: God Can Do the Impossible* (Ann Arbor: Servant Books, 2002).

To experience the healing power of Jesus for all kinds of physical ailments and spiritual needs, there are fundamental requirements:

+ *Make your request in prayer and be persistent.* All of us experience physical and spiritual challenges along the way in life. To put the healing power of Jesus at work in us begins with making a prayer and petition to Our Lord. St. Paul describes this simply: "Have no anxiety at all, but in everything, by prayer and petition, with thanksgiving, make your requests known to God. Then the peace of God that surpasses all understanding will guard your hearts and minds in Christ Jesus" (Phil. 4:6-7).

+ *Have unwavering faith.* A prayer and petition without faith is useless. St. Mark informs us, "Therefore I tell you, all that you ask for in prayer, believe that you will receive it and it shall be yours" (Mark 11:24). St. Matthew writes about the importance of faith as well. He states, "Jesus said to them in reply, 'Amen, I say to you, if you have faith and do not waver, not only will you do what has been done to the fig tree, but even if you say to this mountain, "Be lifted up and thrown into the sea," it will be done'" (Matt. 21:21).

+ *Patience is a must.* In our world today, most people expect their requests to be answered immediately. Our Lord controls the timeline as to when and if He grants our request. A beggar blind from birth was healed (John 9:1-7). A lady with a blood disorder was cured twelve years after she had developed the disease (Luke 8:43-48).

+ *Walk away from temptation and sin.* Earlier we discussed the modern-day healer Sr. Briege McKenna. She said that many of our diseases are rooted in the sickness of our soul. Walk away from temptation and sin to open the door for healing.

✦ *Offer thanksgiving.* We often take for granted the many blessings Jesus provides for us each day. This is a mistake! Our Lord wants us to thank Him regularly for all He does for us, especially for miraculous healings. During His public ministry, Jesus healed ten lepers. Only one of them came back to Jesus and offered thanksgiving for the miracle. At the time, Jesus said, "Ten were cleansed, were they not? Where are the other nine?" (Luke 17:17).

Keep in mind that there will always be naysayers and doubters who challenge the healing power of Jesus. Ignore them! At the time Jesus healed a blind man, restoring his sight, the Pharisees rejected the healing and manufactured ways to downplay it. They complained that Jesus did not keep the Sabbath but performed the miracle on the day of rest. They even questioned the parents of the man as to whether he was truly born blind. However, the former blind man challenged these naysayers, saying, "I told you already and you did not listen.... It is unheard of that anyone ever opened the eyes of a person born blind. If this man were not from God, he would not be able to do anything" (John 9:27, 32–33).

The angel Gabriel said it best about the healing power of God. He told our Blessed Mother Mary that nothing is impossible for God (Luke 1:37). Healings and miracles happen every day whether supernatural, physical, or spiritual. All requests for healing are possible. There are numerous intercessors who have direct contact with God. All we have to do is fulfill the requirements to make a request for a healing in prayer and be persistent, have unwavering faith, exercise patience, walk away from temptation and sin, and offer thanksgiving. There are no guarantees that our requests will be granted, but God is always there listening to us. Always keep in mind that He will always give us the grace and peace that we need to manage any challenges that we may encounter.

Spiritual Treasures for Reflection

For nothing will be impossible for God. (Luke 1:37)

Have no anxiety at all, but in everything, by prayer and petition, with thanksgiving, make your requests known to God. Then the peace of God that surpasses all understanding will guard your hearts and minds in Christ Jesus. (Phil. 4:6–7)

Therefore I tell you, all that you ask for in prayer, believe that you will receive it and it shall be yours. (Mark 11:24)

Teaching #15

Heaven Is the Only Goal in Life

Grace from God: Finding the proper balance
between earthly endeavors and spiritual works

In 2007, a movie titled *The Bucket List* was released. It featured
two terminally ill men around seventy years old staying in the
same hospital room. One was a billionaire, the other a car me-
chanic. Both men developed a bucket list of goals they wanted
to accomplish before they die. Against the advice of their physicians, they left the hospital and began an adventure to pursue
these goals, which included skydiving from an airplane and
visiting special places such as the pyramids, the Taj Mahal, and
the French Riviera. The men had a wonderful time together on
their journey.

Bucket lists have become popular in our American culture.
There are websites dedicated to the best things to do before you
pass from this life. These lists focus only on earthly goals to accomplish. It is common to hear people discuss the goals on their
bucket lists. What about a spiritual bucket list? It has only one

goal—*to reach Heaven*. Working toward spending eternity in Heaven must be the top priority for our time in this life.

Jesus specifically tells us that His goal for us is to reach Heaven. He says, "In my Father's house there are many dwelling places. If there were not, would I have told you that I am going to prepare a place for you? And if I go and prepare a place for you, I will come back again and take you to myself, so that where I am you also may be" (John 14:2–3). St. Paul endorses the statement of Jesus as to our focus in this life. He wrote, "If then you were raised with Christ, seek what is above, where Christ is seated at the right hand of God. Think of what is above, not of what is on earth" (Col. 3:1–2). Also, "Heaven is the ultimate end and fulfillment of the deepest human longings" (CCC 1024).

Why is Heaven the only true goal in life? Because it is the state of supreme, definitive happiness (CCC 1024). Unlike this earthly life, there will be no more tears, death, mourning, wailing, or pain (Rev. 21:4). In Heaven, we are with God, Jesus, the Holy Spirit, our Blessed Mother Mary, the angels, and all of the saints (CCC 1024, 1025). The blessed continue to pursue the will of God in Heaven in relation to others there and to all creation. They reign with Christ forever and ever (CCC 1029).

In Heaven, we will have jobs to perform. St. Thérèse of Lisieux tells us that she will spend her Heaven doing good on earth.[51] Mother Angelica said one of the spiritual works in Heaven will be to pray for those we dearly love on earth who are making mistakes and going in the wrong direction, away from Our Lord. We will try to help move them in the right direction. Mother Angelica

---

[51] St. Thérèse of Lisieux, *Her Last Conversations*, trans. John Clarke, O.C.D. (Washington, DC: ICS Publications, 1977), July 17, 1897, 102.

says, "We will be up there fighting against the enemies of God, not with the weapons of war that destroy but with the weapons of goodness and compassion and love."[52]

At the end of life, every soul will face Jesus one-on-one for our particular judgment (CCC 1051). We will get only one interview. Our life will be reviewed by Our Lord based on our faith and works (CCC 1021, 1059). We will have to render an account for our actions (Matt. 12:36). Jesus will pass judgment on us, either resulting in entrance into heaven immediately, or through a purification process in purgatory, or resulting in immediate and everlasting damnation (CCC 1022, 1030). All who are assigned to purgatory are assured of their eternal salvation (CCC 1030). In purgatory, souls undergo purification "so as to achieve the holiness necessary to enter the joy of heaven" (CCC 1030, 1054).

We must be vigilant in our preparations for our Judgment Day, as Our Lord tells us that we must be like servants waiting for their Master's return from a wedding, always ready to greet Him. For those who are vigilant doing His will on His arrival, Our Lord will receive them. Those who engage in misconduct, the Master will punish severely and assign them a place with the unfaithful. We all must be prepared, for we do not know when the Son of Man will come (Luke 12:35–46).

Consequences for our conduct on earth are described by Jesus in the story of the rich man and Lazarus. The rich man had the best of everything in this earthly life. Lazarus was covered in sores and was so hungry he would eat scraps from the tables of others. When these men died, Lazarus went to the bosom of Abraham,

---

[52] Mother Angelica, "Our Holy Work Will Continue in Heaven," *Catholic Exchange*, June 27, 2019, https://catholicexchange.com/our-holy-work-will-continue-in-heaven/.

and the rich man was brought to the netherworld. The rich man cried out, "Father Abraham, have pity on me. Send Lazarus to dip the tip of his finger in water and cool my tongue, for I am suffering torment in these flames." Abraham replied, "My child, remember that you received what was good during your lifetime while Lazarus likewise received what was bad; but now he is comforted here, whereas you are tormented. Moreover, between us and you a great chasm is established to prevent anyone from crossing who might wish to go from our side to yours or from your side to ours" (Luke 16:19-26).

How do we get there? Jesus tells us that He is the way, the truth, and the life. No one comes to the Father except through Him (John 14:6). Our Lord is the life, as He holds the power to determine who gets to eternity in Heaven on our individual Judgment Day. St. Peter, the first pope of the Church, tells us we are to be living stones following Jesus. He wrote, "Come to him, a living stone, rejected by human beings but chosen and precious in the sight of God, and, like living stones, let yourselves be built into a spiritual house … to offer spiritual sacrifices acceptable to God through Jesus Christ" (1 Pet. 2:4-5).

Jesus wants every soul to make the cut to be with Him in Heaven for eternity. He encourages us to strive hard to get there. Not all will make it, as the gate is narrow. There are no free passes. It is a merit-based system.

There are simple requirements to get there. We must strive to do Our Lord's will and not our own. We can accomplish this by learning His ways of life and living them (see teachings #1-13). This simple truth makes life so much more understandable and enjoyable because we know the way.

Jesus gives us plenty of chances to enter through the narrow gate. In Luke's Gospel, Our Lord tells us the parable of the barren fruit tree. The owner of an orchard complained to his gardener that a fig tree had not produced fruit for three years. The owner instructed the gardener to cut the tree down. However, the gardener requested that the owner give the tree another year that he would cultivate and fertilize it, as it may bear fruit. The gardener further responded that if there was no fruit the next year, the owner could cut it down (Luke 13:6-9). Just as the owner gave the fruit tree another chance to produce, so Our Lord gives us many opportunities to produce for Him.

Our Lord sends us many messengers along the way to guide us and keep us on the right path. There are parents, family members, teachers, priests, neighbors, coaches, or friends who are there for us. They are holy role models seeking to cultivate our souls. Please don't ignore them, as Jesus intentionally sent them directly to you.

Along the way in life, Jesus will discipline us for our misconduct to get our attention. St. Paul tells us, "My son, do not disdain the discipline of the Lord or lose heart when reproved by him; for whom the Lord loves, he disciplines.... Endure your trials as 'discipline'; God treats you as sons. For what 'son' is there whom his Father does not discipline?" (Heb. 12:5-7). He further explains to us that this discipline may be painful now, yet later it brings great fruit to those who are trained by it (Heb. 12:11).

For many of us, our focus is on earthly goals. One of them is to acquire material things, such as a great home, new cars, a boat, or fashionable clothes. For some, the pursuit of power over others consumes them, whether in business or government. Still others seek to acquire the latest devices, such as cell phones, computers, and smart televisions. We can't seem to live without continuous entertainment from television shows, social media, and the latest news. Another goal is to leave the work force early with a huge retirement plan to live comfortably for the rest of our lives. It seems that we will stop at nothing and do whatever it takes to reach these goals. Often this includes ignoring the obligations to raise our families or stepping over the line of moral and ethical boundaries.

Accomplishing some or all of these goals provides only temporary satisfaction. Once we achieve one goal, we focus our attention on the next one. We get on this treadmill of short- and long-term goal accomplishments which can consume our lives.

What is wrong with this picture? There is no emphasis on spiritual actions to reach the long-term goal of Heaven. This goal has taken a back seat to earthly pursuits. Jesus directly addresses this issue. He says, "Do not store up for yourselves treasures on earth, where moth and decay destroy, and thieves break in and steal. But store up treasures in heaven, where neither moth nor decay destroys, nor thieves break in and steal. For where your treasure is, there also will your heart be." Our Lord further tells us, "No one can serve two masters. He will either hate one and love the other, or be devoted to one and despise the other. You cannot serve God and mammon" (Matt. 6:19–21, 24).

As we know from our knowledge of Judgment Day, faith and good works lead to eternal salvation. Sure, we can enjoy some of the fruits of this earthly life, but we can't do so to the extent of the exclusion of our spiritual life. Prayer time, weekly attendance at Mass or more often, participating in the sacraments, and spiritual reading have to be part of our daily routines. Spending some of our time in ministry work, giving back to the Lord for all the blessings He has bestowed on us, must be part of our focus. Balance is the difference between living an abundant life or one with a misguided focus and being bounced around like a ping-pong ball from temporary joy to unhappiness.

Jesus wants us to live an abundant life which features a balanced combination of earthly and spiritual actions and goals. Jesus said, "I came so that they might have life and have it more abundantly" (John 10:10). The simple message is this: even the best day on earth pales by comparison to eternal life in heaven.

Before the Last Judgment, there will be a resurrection of all the dead. This is the time when all souls will hear the Son of Man's voice. For those who have been good, they will experience the resurrection of life. The souls who have been evil will have the resurrection of judgment. Then Jesus will come in all His glory with the angels, and He will separate the good from the wicked. The righteous will be awarded eternal life. The wicked will be given eternal punishment (CCC 1038).

The Father will determine the time of the Last Judgment. At this time, God's justice will triumph over all the injustices committed by us. Jesus will have the final word on all of history. We will gain an understanding of the whole work of creation and of how His providence led everything to the final end (CCC 1040).

The disclosure of the Last Judgment is to give all souls the opportunity to convert while there is still time. We must commit to God's ways and have a holy fear of Him (CCC 1041).

So many of us in our world today spend our lives seeking earthly goals of material things, power, entertainment, and wealth for retirement. These goals are misguided, as they only lead to temporary joy. Our focus must be on the one true spiritual goal to reach Heaven. It is there we will reach supreme, definitive happiness to be with Our Lord forever and ever.

Spiritual Treasures for Reflection

In my Father's house there are many dwelling places. If there were not, would I have told you that I am going to prepare a place for you? And if I go and prepare a place for you, I will come back again and take you to myself, so that where I am you also may be. (John 14:2–3)

I tell you, on the day of judgment people will render an account for every careless word they speak. (Matt. 12:36)

My son, do not disdain the discipline of the Lord or lose heart when reproved by him; for whom the Lord loves, he disciplines. (Heb. 12:5–6)

Reflection Questions on Each
of the Teachings of Jesus

#1. LOVE GOD WITHOUT LIMITS

✦ *How can we build a strong relationship with God?*

✦ *What does it mean for us to be
a handmaid of the Lord?*

✦ *Since God loves us without limits, why
can't we love Him in the same way?*

#2. LOVE YOUR NEIGHBOR AS YOURSELF

✦ *What does it mean to be selfless?*

✦ *Is there a greater joy in life than helping others
in need? Please explain your answer.*

✦ *Why can't we love others without reservation,
in the same way God loves us?*

#3. Eliminate Temptation and Sin from Your Life

✦ *Who is going to win the race for your soul—God or the enemy?*

✦ *What tools can we use to ensure that God's will is the winner in the race for our souls?*

✦ *Should we use our God-given tools daily or wait until we are at our weakest point?*

#4. Listen to the Voice of Jesus

✦ *Why is it important to learn to listen to the voice of Jesus?*

✦ *What are the avenues available to us to listen to the voice of Our Lord?*

✦ *What is the process to follow to make good decisions in all our actions?*

#5 Faith Is a Necessity, Not an Option

✦ *What are examples of direct and circumstantial proof that Jesus is real?*

✦ *Does faith produce perseverance in our most challenging times? Please explain your answer.*

✦ *What prevents us from having our faith operate on autopilot with unwavering trust in Jesus?*

#6. DIVINE PEACE IS THE REMEDY FOR FEAR, STRESS, WORRY, AND ANXIETY

+ *What were the first words Jesus spoke to the apostles in the upper room on the day of His Resurrection?*

+ *Describe the four-step process to follow to eliminate fear, stress, worry, and anxiety from our lives.*

+ *How did Jesus use the four-step process when He was in the Garden of Gethsemane?*

#7. REPLACE SPIRITUAL MEDIOCRITY WITH SPIRITUAL MATURITY

+ *What role is the Holy Spirit to play in our lives?*

+ *What are the gifts and fruits of the Holy Spirit that are at work in us?*

+ *How do we activate the Holy Spirit to work in our souls?*

#8. BE A CATALYST FOR JESUS: TEACH OTHERS HIS VALUES TO HELP THEM REACH HEAVEN

+ *Who was the greatest catalyst for spiritual change in the world?*

+ *What was the purpose of Jesus' sending out the seventy-two disciples to do public ministry?*

+ *How can we be catalysts for others in the world around us to help them reach Heaven?*

#9. The Eucharist and Confession Are the Highways to Heaven

+ *Is it important to spend time daily developing a healthy spiritual life? Please explain your answer.*

+ *What are some of the miracles that prove that the Eucharist is the Real Presence of Jesus?*

+ *What are the effects of the Eucharist on our souls?*

+ *What are the effects of the Sacrament of Confession on our souls?*

#10. Devotion to Our Blessed Mother Mary

+ *What is the goal of our Blessed Mother Mary for every soul?*

+ *What is holding us back from responding to Our Lady's call to "Do whatever He tells you"?*

+ *How can we build a strong relationship with Mary, our Mother, to experience her many graces, blessings, and intercessions?*

#11. PRAYER TIME WITH JESUS IS THE MOST IMPORTANT TIME OF THE DAY

✦ *What are the fundamentals of a strong prayer life?*

✦ *What are some of the ways
we can broaden our prayer life?*

✦ *How do we build a mature relationship
with our Savior, Jesus?*

#12. MODELING OUR FAMILIES AFTER THE VALUES OF THE HOLY FAMILY

✦ *What are the fundamental elements of a holy family?*

✦ *What are the duties of parents in raising their children?*

✦ *Describe the benefits for families who practice
the fundamental elements of a holy family.*

#13. MANAGING THE TWO ELEPHANTS IN THE ROOM: SUFFERING AND DEATH

✦ *What are the tools that Jesus
gave us to manage suffering?*

✦ *Can managing suffering the way
Jesus did make us holy?*

✦ Why is it important to be prepared for
the end of our earthly lives?

✦ How can we build up our spiritual résumé so we
will be ready when Jesus calls us from this life?

#14. EXPERIENCE THE MIRACULOUS HEALING
POWER OF GOD, THE DIVINE PHYSICIAN

✦ Are all things possible for God?
Please explain your answer.

✦ What are the different types of miracles?

✦ What are the fundamental requirements to
experience the healing power of Jesus?

#15. HEAVEN IS THE ONLY GOAL IN LIFE

✦ Why is Heaven the only true goal in life?

✦ What are the requirements to gain Heaven?

✦ Should our focus in life be on earthly
accomplishments or on spiritual actions?

Part III

Answering Your Call from Jesus – Developing a Master Plan to Live the Values of Jesus in Order to Reach Heaven

For over forty years, a ten-thousand-meter road race known as the Crescent City Classic has been held in New Orleans on the Saturday of Easter weekend. The race attracts runners from all over the country. Typically, there are over twenty thousand entrants each year. To run the race successfully, it is important that participants develop and follow a master plan. This plan consists of training on a daily basis, beginning with running short distances and gradually working up stamina to be able to complete ten thousand meters. The training period can be as little as one month or longer, depending upon the condition and experience of the runner. On race day, there is great joy and excitement in the atmosphere for all participants. A master plan is a must to reach the goal of finishing the race successfully.

The end goal of every soul should be to reach Heaven. We don't get there by accident. We must develop a master plan, answering the call from Jesus to live His ways and follow them. This concept is not rocket science. Developing a master plan as guided by the

Holy Spirit only takes fifteen to twenty minutes. Our eternity in Heaven is certainly worth the effort to develop and follow a plan.

Before Jesus came into the world, the mindset of many people of the time was of hopelessness. Job described this attitude when he wrote that man's life on earth is a drudgery and without hope. He was discouraged that he would not see happiness again (Job 7:1–7). The only hope was for the Messiah to enter the world (Isa. 42:1, 4).

Recognizing the state of life on earth, God implemented His master plan to save mankind by sending His Son, Jesus, into the world as our Savior. At His baptism at age thirty, Our Lord began His public ministry to save us in a spectacular way. During this event, the Holy Spirit descended upon Jesus like a dove, and God spoke from the heavens, saying, "This is my beloved Son, with whom I am well pleased" (Matt. 3:17).

Jesus continued to implement the master plan of His Father by performing many miracles of healing the sick, raising the dead, changing the weather, and feeding five thousand people. Further, He taught us His ways of life and lived them without sin. Jesus fulfilled God's master plan for Him on earth by His Crucifixion, Resurrection, and Ascension into Heaven. Also, He sent the Holy Spirit to the apostles and gave them divine peace on the day of His Resurrection.

Our Lord has a master plan for each soul born into the world. St. Paul describes this plan for us: "For we are his handiwork, created in Christ Jesus for the good works that God has prepared in advance, that we should live in them" (Eph. 2:10). These individual plans begin with His calling every soul by spiritual lightning at some time in their life. Each soul has to make a decision to answer this call to learn and live Our Lord's ways or ignore it. If we answer the call from Jesus, we must develop a master plan for our souls—to live the values of Jesus in order to reach Heaven. Since God utilized a master plan for His Son to save mankind, why can't we develop and implement His master plan for our souls?

Sadly, we have varying levels of acceptance of Our Lord's plan for us. For some, the pursuit of this plan is a full-time endeavor doing the Lord's will always. For others, the response is only lukewarm, where at times we allow our will to yield to the temptations of the earthly world of pride, greed, gluttony, anger, lust, envy, laziness, or other misconduct. There is a third group of souls who ignore the call entirely and risk the loss of Heaven. St. Peter encourages us to pursue our master plan. He wrote, "Therefore, brothers, be all the more eager to make your call and election firm, for, in doing so, you will never stumble. For, in this way, entry into the eternal kingdom of our Lord and savior Jesus Christ will be richly provided for you" (2 Pet. 1:10–11).

Jesus needs to be at first place in our lives. He tells us, "So be perfect, just as your heavenly Father is perfect" (Matt. 5:48).

A master plan consists of living the ways of Jesus:

1. *Love God without limits by . . .*

+ *Daily Prayer:* There are many ways to pray, such as rote prayers, time alone with Jesus in a quiet place at home or in Adoration in a church or chapel, or doing the daily Ignatian Examen. Examples of rote prayers include the Our Father, Rosary, Memorare, Chaplet of Divine Mercy, Litanies, Angelus, and Prayer to St. Michael the Archangel.

+ *Partaking of the Sacraments:* Attendance at Mass on Sundays or during the week to receive the Eucharist. Holy Communion is the bread of the strong, for which we can draw courage and strength each day.[53] The Sacrament of

---

[53] St. Faustina, *Diary* 91.

Reconciliation (Confession) is the opportunity to purify our souls from the burden of sin, receive mercy from Jesus for our misconduct, and restore divine peace in our hearts. If you haven't participated in the sacrament for a long time, go now and revive your soul.

2. *Love your neighbor as yourself.* In our culture today, much of the focus of our daily activities is doing what is best for "me." Our Lord has taught us that we are to be more concerned with the needs of others, being selfless rather than being selfish and only focused on ourselves. We can fulfill this teaching by volunteering our time in church ministry or community projects or helping children, the poor, our neighbors, the marginalized, and those who are victims.

3. *Imitate the Holy Family.* Families must practice the Christian values of prayer, self-discipline, great work ethic, sacrifice, and love as demonstrated by the Holy Family. This means spending quality undistracted time together each day, praying at meals and at bedtime, doing chores, caring for the needs of family members, and nurturing children to be prepared for adulthood. By engaging in the practice of these values and activities, families will have strong bonds together and experience great joy.

4. *Eliminate temptation and sin.* All of us have one or more weaknesses in our souls. Spend some time analyzing your soul and identify them. Utilize the tools of practicing virtues, self-discipline, the daily examen, the daily scorecard, and the Sacrament of Confession to terminate these weaknesses.

5. *Listen to the voice of Jesus.* The commandment to listen to the voice of Jesus comes from God. When Peter, James, and John were on Mount Tabor, Jesus was transfigured into His Divine Being. God told those apostles to listen to His Son (Luke 9:35). Listening to the voice of Jesus is a must for all of our daily actions, as confirmed by St. Paul, Elijah, and the psalmist David. Our Lord

spent His life on earth listening to the direction of His Father. Rote prayers, Adoration time, spiritual reading of the Bible or books on Christianity are simple ways to give us access to His voice. Jesus is there for us at all times. All we have to do is to reach out to Him.

6. *Teach others the values of Jesus to help them get to Heaven.* Jesus was the greatest catalyst for spiritual change. He desperately wants His teachings to reach all souls so they can reach heaven. After He was crucified, He commanded us to go out into the whole world and proclaim the Gospel to every creature (Mark 16:15). Spreading the Good News begins at home in our families and continues with everyone we communicate with, such as work colleagues, friends, neighbors, educators, students, those in ministry, and all others. Participate in church ministries and pray for those who are suffering. The priest gives us his final blessing at Mass, saying, "Go and announce the Gospel of the Lord."

In our work life, nearly all of us have been required to submit an application or a résumé for a job. It typically consists of our past education and work history, list of skills, awards/honors, and references. The purpose is for an employer to make a hiring decision. Similarly, a master plan is comparable to an employment application for a job. Instead of making a decision about employment, Our Lord will review our performance as to our master plan in order to consider admitting us to Heaven by looking at whether we did His will by following His ways. It is undisputed that our principal purpose in life is to serve Him and not ourselves, using all the talents He gave us.

It is most important to develop a personal master plan and follow it. Our performance will be reviewed by Our Lord when He calls us from this life. After all, when we face Jesus on our Judgment Day, we want Him to say, "Well done, my good and faithful servant.... Come, share your master's joy" (Matt. 25:23). We don't want His response to be, "You wicked, lazy servant!... Throw this useless servant into the darkness outside, where there will be wailing and grinding of teeth" (Matt. 25:26, 30).

At different points in our lives, Jesus calls us to live His ways to help us reach Heaven. A common question that comes with His call is "What does God want me to do with my life?" Spending fifteen to twenty minutes developing your master plan gives you the response to His call and answers the question of what He wants you to do. We must say *yes* to this call.

The prophet Isaiah sums up the whole issue of answering the call from Jesus. He wrote:

I, the LORD, have called you
   for justice,
I have grasped you by the hand;
I formed you, and set you
as a covenant for the people,
a light for the nations,
To open the eyes of the blind,
to bring out prisoners from confinement,
and from the dungeon, those who live in darkness (42:6–7).

My Master Plan for Jesus

1. *Love God without limits and listen to His voice.*

Daily prayer: rote prayers such as the Our Father, the Rosary, the Chaplet of Divine Mercy, litanies, the Memorare, the Angelus, and the Prayer to St. Michael the Archangel.

When: _____

Adoration time

When: _____

Reflection time with Jesus, including the Ignatian examen

When: _____

Partaking of the sacraments

Mass/Eucharist—When: _____

Confession—When: _____

2. *Love your neighbor as yourself and teach others the values of Jesus to help them get to Heaven.*

Help others: including family, friends, and the poor—through ministry or community activities, or both.

Identify action items: _____

_____

_____

When: _____

3. *Imitate the Holy Family.*

Undistracted quality family time: at meals, bedtime, chores, and activities together.

Identify action items: _____

When: _____

4. *Eliminate temptation and sin.*

Identify a weakness or two to terminate by using the tools of practicing virtues, self-discipline, the daily examen, the daily scorecard, and Confession.

Identify the sin(s): _____

Tools to use from part II, teaching #3 _____

_____

_____

5. *Spiritual reading to grow in your faith*

Suggested materials: New American Bible (any one of the Gospels), *Introduction to the Spiritual Life* by Brant Pitre; *Mother Angelica's Little Book of Life Lessons and Everyday Spirituality* by Raymond Arroyo, *Always Discerning* by Fr. Joseph Tetlow, and *The Lamb's Supper* by Scott Hahn.

What book: _____

When: _____

About the Author

Richard Eason has been a permanent deacon in the Archdiocese of New Orleans since 2012 and is assigned to Good Shepherd Parish. He participates in several Catholic apostolates, including being on the board of directors of the Ozanam Inn homeless shelter, being on the advisory board of St. Michael Special School, and volunteering at St. Jude Nursing Home in New Orleans, and he serves in the community as a member of the ForeKids! Foundation. He is also a frequent speaker on spiritual excellence (as a series and study group) in Catholic parishes and prayer groups. The title of his first book is *Spiritual Excellence: The Path to Happiness, Holiness, and Heaven.*

Deacon Richard graduated with honors from Tulane University with a degree in economics and from Loyola University New Orleans School of Law. He practices as a civil litigator with the regional law firm of Adams and Reese, LLC. He has served on the firm's executive committee and as a practice group leader for the litigation team. He has extensive trial experience in complex commercial and personal injury cases in state and U.S. district courts in Louisiana, Texas, and Mississippi. He has appeared before the U.S. 5th and 11th circuit courts of appeal and the U.S. Supreme Court.

Deacon Eason is blessed to be married to his wife, Rosalyn, and to have three sons, Blake, Kyle, and Grant; a daughter-in-law, Ashley; a future daughter-in-law, Jenn Travis; and two wonderful grandchildren, Evan and Clare.